Gynocentrism

From Feudalism to Feminism

Peter Wright

Preface

Gynocentrism, a centuries old term, refers to the principle of female centeredness or female dominance in various social or interpersonal contexts.

The term has recently enjoyed a resurgence, serving again as a descriptor of the expanding yet centuries old obsession with the rights, status, and power of women. This book traces the history of that tradition to its roots in medieval society, while being careful to note the difference between benign gynocentric acts and the more problematic examples of gynocentric culture.

The essays collected in this volume were originally penned as separate pieces for the website *Gynocentrism and its Cultural Origins*, and have since been revised for this paperback edition. There are several repetitions of comments and quotes for which I apologize and ask the reader's grace – they are integral to the structure of the articles and for that purpose have been retained.

The essays are grouped into five parts exploring various aspects of gynocentrism, and providing examples of the phenomenon from historical literature. The final part, *Post Gynocentric Relationships* explores the possibility of relationships built on the notion of friendship as an alternative to neurotic shibboleths of romantic love.

Peter Wright, August 2014.

Table of Contents

PREFACE

PART ONE: About Gynocentrism

1. Introduction to Gynocentrism
2. Gynocentric Culture
3. Timeline of Gynocentric Culture
4. La Querelle des Femmes
5, Romantic Writing as Medium

PART TWO: The Structure of Gynocentrism

6. Gynocentric Chivalry
7. 'Frau Minne' The Goddess Who Steals Men's Hearts
8. The Sexual-Relations Contract
9. Damseling, Chivalry and Courtly Love
10. Taming Men for Women and State
11. Gynocentrism as a Narcissistic Pathology
12. A Sentimental Continuation of Coverture

PART THREE: Rituals of Romance

13. The Art of Attraction
14. Valentine's Day
15. The Rituals of Marriage
16. Down the Aisle Again

PART FOUR: The Status Quo

17. What Happened to Chivalry?
18. Feminism – The Same Old Story
19. Gynocentrism: Why So Hard To Kill?

PART FIVE: Post Gynocentric Relationships

20. Sex and Attachment
21. Romantic Love, or Friendship?
22. Pleasure-seeking vs. Relationships
23. Don't Just Do Something, SIT THERE

PART ONE

About Gynocentrism

1. Introduction to Gynocentrism

Gynocentrism n. (Greek, γυνή, "female" – Latin *centrum*, "centred") refers to a dominant or exclusive focus on women in theory or practice; or to the advocacy of this.[1] Anything can be considered gynocentric (Adj.) when it is concerned exclusively with a female (or specifically a feminist) point of view.[2]

Introduction

Cultural gynocentrism arose in Medieval Europe during a period cross-cultural influences and momentous changes in gendered customs. Beginning in around the 12th century European society birthed an intersection of Arabic practices of female worship, aristocratic courting trends, the Marian cult, along with the imperial patronage of Eleanor of Aquitaine and her daughter Marie De Champagne who together crafted the military notion of chivalry into a notion of servicing ladies, a practice otherwise known as 'courtly love.'

Courtly love was enacted by minstrels, playrights and troubadours, and especially via hired romance-writers like Chrétien de Troyes and Andreas Capellanus who laid down a model of romantic fiction that is still the biggest grossing genre of literature today. That confluence of factors generated the cultural conventions that continue to drive gynocentrism today.

Gynocentrism as a cultural phenomenon

The primary elements of gynocentric culture, as we experience it today, are derived from practices originating in medieval society such as feudalism, chivalry and courtly love that continue to inform contemporary society in subtle ways. Such gynocentric patters constitute a "sexual feudalism," as attested by female writers like Lucrezia Marinella who in 1600 AD recounted that women of lower socioeconomic classes were treated as superiors by men who acted as servants or beasts born to serve them, or by Modesta Pozzo who in 1590 wrote;

> "don't we see that men's rightful task is to go out to work and wear themselves out trying to accumulate wealth, as though they were our factors or stewards, so that we can remain at home like the lady of the house directing their work and enjoying the profit of their labors? That, if you like, is the reason why men are naturally stronger and more robust than us — they need to be, so they can put up with the hard labor they must endure in our service."[3]

The golden casket above depicting scenes of servile behaviour toward women were typical of courtly love culture of the Middle Ages. Such objects were given to women as gifts by men seeking to impress. Note the woman standing with hands on hips in a position of authority, and the man being led around by a neck halter, his hands clasped in a position of subservience.

It's clear that much of what we today call gynocentrism was invented in the Middle Ages with the cultural practices of romantic chivalry and courtly love. In 12th century Europe, feudalism served as the basis for a new model for love in which men were to play the role of vassal to women who played the role of an idealized Lord. C.S. Lewis, back in the middle of the 20th Century, referred to this historical revolution as "the feudalisation of love," and stated that it has left no corner of our ethics, our imagination, or our daily life untouched. "Compared with this revolution," states Lewis, "the Renaissance is a mere ripple on the surface of literature."[4] Lewis further states;

> "Everyone has heard of courtly love, and everyone knows it appeared quite suddenly at the end of the eleventh century at Languedoc. The sentiment, of course, is love, but love of a highly specialized sort, whose characteristics may be enumerated as Humility, Courtesy, and the Religion of Love. The lover is always abject. Obedience to his lady's lightest wish, however whimsical, and silent acquiescence in her rebukes, however unjust, are the only virtues he dares to claim. Here is a service of love closely modelled on the service which a feudal vassal owes to his lord. The lover is the lady's 'man'. He addresses her as *midons*, which etymologically represents not 'my lady' but 'my lord'. The whole attitude has been rightly described as 'a feudalisation of love'. This solemn amatory ritual is felt to be part and parcel of the courtly life." [5]

With the advent of (initially courtly) women being elevated to the position of 'Lord' in intimate relationships, and with this general sentiment diffusing to the masses and across much of the world today, we are justified in talking of a gynocentric cultural complex that affects, among other things, relationships between men and women. Further, unless evidence of widespread gynocentric culture can be found prior to the Middle Ages, then gynocentrism is precisely 800 years old. In order to determine if this thesis is valid we need to look further at what we mean by "gynocentrism".

The term gynocentrism has been in circulation since the 1800's, with the general definition being "focused on women; concerned with only women." [6] From this definition we see that gynocentrism could refer to any female-centered practice, or to a single gynocentric act carried out by one individual. There is nothing inherently wrong with a gynocentric act (eg. celebrating Mother's Day) , or for that matter an androcentric act (celebrating Father's Day). However when a given act becomes instituted in the culture to the exclusion of other acts we are then dealing with a hegemonic custom — i.e. such is the relationship custom of elevating women to the position of men's social, moral or spiritual superiors.

Author of Gynocentrism Theory Adam Kostakis has attempted to expand the definition of gynocentrism to refer to "male sacrifice for the benefit of women" and "the deference of men to women," and he concludes; "Gynocentrism, whether it went by the name honor, nobility, chivalry, or feminism, its essence has gone unchanged. It remains a peculiarly male duty to help the women onto the lifeboats, while the men themselves face a certain and icy death." [7]

While we can agree with Kostakis' descriptions of assumed male duty, the phrase *gynocentric culture* more accurately carries his intention than *gynocentrism* alone. Thus when used alone in the context of this book gynocentrism refers to part or all of gynocentric culture, which is defined here as *any culture instituting rules for gender relationships that benefit females at the expense of males across a broad range of measures.*

At the base of gynocentric culture lies the practice of enforced male sacrifice for the benefit of women. If we accept this definition we must look back and ask whether male sacrifices throughout history were *always* made for the sake women, or alternatively for the sake of some other primary goal? For instance, when men went to die in vast numbers in wars, was it for women, or was it rather for Man, King, God and Country? If the latter we cannot then claim that this was a result of some intentional gynocentric culture, at least not in the way I have defined it here. If the sacrifice isn't intended directly for the benefit women, even if women were occasional beneficiaries of male sacrifice, then we are not dealing with gynocentric culture.

Male utility and disposability strictly "for the benefit of women" comes in strongly only after the advent of the 12th century gender revolution in Europe – a revolution that delivered us terms like gallantry, chivalry, chivalric love, courtesy, damsels, romance and so on. From that period onward gynocentric practices grew exponentially, culminating in the demands of today's feminist movement. In sum, gynocentrism (ie. gynocentric culture) was a patchy phenomenon at best before the middle ages, after which it became ubiquitous.

With this in mind it makes little sense to talk of gynocentric culture starting with the industrial revolution a mere 200 years ago (or 100 or even 30 yrs ago), or of it being two million years old as some would argue. We are not only fighting two million years of genetic programming; our culturally constructed problem of gender inequity is much simpler to pinpoint and to potentially reverse. All we need do is look at the circumstances under which gynocentric culture first began to flourish and attempt to reverse those circumstances. Specifically, that means rejecting the illusions of romantic love (feudalised love), along with the practices of misandry, male shaming and servitude that ultimately support it.

La Querelle des Femmes, and advocacy for women

The *Querelle des Femmes* translates as the "quarrel about women" and amounts to what we might today call a gender-war. The *querelle* had its beginning in twelfth century Europe and finds its culmination in the feminist-driven ideology of today (though some authors claim, unconvincingly, that the *querelle* came to an end in the 1700s). The basic theme of the centuries-long quarrel revolved, and continues to revolve, around advocacy for the rights, power and status of women, and thus *Querelle des Femmes* serves as the originating title for gynocentric discourse.

If we consider the longevity of this revolution we might be inclined to agree with Barbarossa's claim "that feminism is a perpetual advocacy machine for women".

To place the above events into a coherent timeline, chivalric servitude toward women was elaborated and given patronage first under the reign of Eleanor of Aquitaine (1137-1152) and instituted culturally throughout Europe over the subsequent 200 year period. After becoming thus entrenched on European soil there arose the *Querelle des Femmes* which refers to the advocacy culture that arose for protecting, perpetuating and increasing female power in relation to men that continues, in an unbroken tradition, in the efforts of contemporary feminism.[8]

Writings from the Middle Ages forward are full of testaments about men attempting to adapt to the feudalisation of love and the serving of women, along with the emotional agony, shame and sometimes physical violence they suffered in the process. Gynocentric chivalry and the associated *querelle* have not received much elaboration in men's studies courses to-date, but with the emergence of new manuscripts and quality English translations it may be profitable to begin blazing this trail.[9]

References

1. Oxford English Dictionary – Vers.4.0 (2009), Oxford University Press, ISBN 978-0199563838
2. Oxford English Dictionary 2010
3. Modesta Pozzo, *The Worth of Women: their Nobility and Superiority to Men*
4. C.S. Lewis, Friendship, chapter in The Four Loves, HarperCollins, 1960
5. C.S. Lewis, The Allegory of Love, Oxford University Press, 1936
6. Dictionary.com – Gynocentric
7. Adam Kostakis, Gynocentrism Theory – (Published online, 2011). Although Kostakis assumes gynocentrism has been around throughout recorded history, he singles out the Middle Ages for comment: *"There is an enormous amount of continuity between the chivalric class code which arose in the Middle Ages and modern feminism… One could say that they are the same entity, which now exists in a more mature form – certainly, we are not dealing with two separate creatures."*
8. Joan Kelly, Early Feminist Theory and the Querelle des Femmes (1982), reprinted in *Women, History and Theory*, UCP (1984)
9. The *New Male Studies Journal* has published thoughtful articles touching on the history and influence of chivalry in the lives of males.

2. Gynocentric culture

Did female-centered culture begin in the prehistoric era?

This question is sometimes asked by people who feel that gynocentrism has been around for the entirety of human evolution. The answer to that question is of course yes – *gynocentrism has been around throughout human history.* However it's important to make a distinction between gynocentrism (that is, individual gynocentric acts, customs, or events) and gynocentric culture (a pervasive cultural complex that affects every aspect of life). We will never be precise enough to make sense of this subject unless we insist on this distinction between gynocentric acts and gynocentric-culture.

Gynocentrism:

It's easy to overstate the import of specific examples of gynocentrism when in fact such examples may be equally balanced, culturally speaking, by male-centered acts, customs, or events which negate the concept of a pervasive gynocentric culture. Here we are reminded of the old adage that one swallow does not make a summer, and that likewise individual gynocentric acts, or even a small collection of such acts, do not amount to a pervasive gynocentric culture.

Individual examples of gynocentrism are sometimes misconstrued as representing a broader culture, as seen in the discussion around ancient female figurines which some claim are indications of goddess-worshipping, gynocentric cultures. Not only is the import of the female figurines vastly overstated, the quantity discovered is potentially exaggerated according to leading feminist archaeologists:

"Quantitative analyses of Upper Palaeolithic imagery make it clear that there are also images of males and that, by and large, most of the imagery of humans-humanoids cannot readily be identified as male or female. In fact, no source can affirm that more than 50 per cent of the imagery is recognizably female." [1]

Even if the majority of these figurines had proven to be female, this wouldn't indicate a gynocentric culture any more than would statues of the goddess Athena and the Parthenon built in her honor indicate that ancient Athens was a gynocentric city – which it clearly was not.

Archaeologists discovered stencils of female hands in ancient caves, created by the practice of spraying mud from the mouth onto a female hand. Some were led to surmise, without evidence, that those same hands served as authorship of the animals that were also painted on the cave walls. Additionally, these archaeologists assumed that the presence of female hand images not only meant that women painted the cave art but that the entire ancient world "must have" consisted of a completely gynocentric culture. These assumptions show the dangers of allowing imagination to depart too far from the evidence.

Further examples of overreach are the citing of fictional material from classical era, such as Helen of Troy (a Greek myth), or Lysistrata (a Greek play) as proof of gynocentric culture; unfortunately these examples are about as helpful for understanding gynocentrism as would be the movie Planet of the Apes to future researchers studying the history of primates.

Gynocentric culture:

A cultural complex refers to a significant configuration of culture traits that have major significance in the way people's lives were lived. In sociology it is defined as a set of culture traits all unified and dominated by one essential trait; such as an industrial cultural complex, religious cultural complex, military cultural complex and so on. In each of these complexes we can identify a core factor – industry, religion, military – so we likewise require a core factor for the gynocentric cultural complex in order for it to qualify for the title. At the core of the gynocentric cultural complex is the feudalistic structure of *lords* and *vassals*, a structure which came to be adopted as a gender relations model requiring men to serve as vassals to women. C.S. Lewis called this restructuring of gender relations 'the feudalisation of love' and rightly suggested that is has left no corner of our ethics, our imagination, or our daily life untouched.

The feudalisation of love was not something seen in pre-medieval times, let alone in the Palaeolithic era when feudalism simply didn't exist. For example, we have not yet seen a cave painting equal to the famous French jewellery box art from the Middle Ages showing a male as subservient vassal to a dominant woman who leads him around by a neck halter.

In summary, it appears everyone agrees that examples of gynocentric acts have existed throughout human history. The question is not whether an act occurred but whether or not it was part of a more dominant culture of gynocentrism. The answer sought is not when a gynocentric act was recorded but when the gynocentric cultural complex (GCC) began, on which point there appear to be three main theories:

► Ancient Genesis
► Medieval Genesis
► Recent Genesis

This book provides evidence that clearly favors Medieval genesis, as there is simply not enough evidence for it in ancient culture beyond scattered examples of gynocentrism. In fact what we do know of classical civilizations appears to favour the reverse conclusion – that these were patently androcentric cultures that held sway globally until the 12th century European revolution.

References:

[1] Lucy Goodison (Editor), Christine Morris (Editor) Ancient Goddesses (Wisconsin Studies in Classics) University of Wisconsin Press (May 14, 1999)

3. Timeline of gynocentric culture

The following timeline details the birth of gynocentric culture along with significant historical events that ensured its survival. Prior to 1200 AD broadspread gynocentric culture simply did not exist, despite evidence of isolated gynocentric acts and events. It was only in the Middle Ages that gynocentrism developed cultural complexity and became a ubiquitous and enduring cultural norm.

1102 AD: Gynocentrism meme first introduced

William IX, Duke of Aquitaine, the most powerful feudal lord in France, wrote the first troubadour poems and is widely considered the first troubadour. Parting with the tradition of fighting wars strictly on behalf of man, king, God and country, William is said to have had the image of his mistress painted on his shield, whom he called midons (my Lord) saying that, "It was his will to bear her in battle, as she had borne him in bed."[1]

1168 – 1198 AD: Gynocentrism meme elaborated, given imperial patronage

The gynocentrism meme is further popularized and given imperial patronage by William's granddaughter Queen Eleanor of Aquitaine and her daughter Marie.[2] At Eleanor's court in Poitiers Eleanor and Marie completed the work of embroidering the Christian military code of chivalry with a code for romantic lovers, thus putting women at the center of courtly life, and placing love on the throne of God himself – and in doing so they had changed the face of chivalry forever. Key events are:

1170 AD: Eleanor and Marie established the formal *Courts of Love* presided over by themselves and a jury of 60 noble ladies who would investigate and hand down judgements on love-disputes according to the newly introduced code governing gender relations. The courts were modelled precisely along the lines of the traditional feudal courts where disputes between retainers had been settled by the powerful lord. In this case however the disputes were between lovers.

1180 AD: Marie directs Chrétien de Troyes to write Lancelot, the Knight of the Cart, a love story about Lancelot and Guinevere elaborating the nature of gynocentric chivalry. Chrétien de Troyes abandoned this project before it was completed because he objected to the implicit approval of the adulterous affair between Lancelot and Guinevere that Marie had directed him to write. But the approval of the legend was irresistible – later poets completed the story on Chrétien's behalf. Chrétien also wrote other famous romances including *Erec* and *Enide*.

1188 AD: Marie directs her chaplain Andreas Capellanus to write *The Art of Courtly Love*. This guide to the chivalric codes of romantic love is a document that could pass as contemporary in almost every respect, excepting for the outdated class structures and assumptions. Many of the admonitions in Andreas "textbook" clearly come from the women who directed the writing.[3]

1180 – 1380 AD: Gynocentric culture spreads throughout Europe

In two hundred years gynocentric culture spread from France to become instituted in all the principle courts of Europe, and from there went on to capture the imagination of men, women and children of all social classes. According to Jennifer Wollock,[4] the continuing popularity of chivalric love stories is also confirmed by the contents of women's libraries of the late Middle Ages, literature which had a substantial female readership including mothers reading to their daughters. Aside from the growing access to literature, gynocentric culture values spread via everyday interactions among people in which they created, shared, and/or exchanged the information and ideas.

1386 AD: Gynocentric concept of 'gentleman' formed

Coined in the 1200's, the word "Gentil man" soon became synonymous with chivalry. According to the Oxford

Dictionary *gentleman* came to refer by 1386 to "a man with chivalrous instincts and fine feelings". Gentleman therefore implies chivalric behaviour and serves as a synonym for it; a meaning that has been retained to the present day.

1400 AD: Beginning of the the Querelle des Femmes

The *Querelle des Femmes* or "quarrel about women" technically had its beginning in 1230 AD with the publication of *Romance of the Rose*. However it was Italian-French author Christine de Pizan who in 1400 AD turned the prevailing discussion about women into a debate that continues to reverberate in feminist ideology today (though some authors claim, unconvincingly, that the *querelle* came to an end in the 1700s). The basic theme of the centuries-long quarrel revolved, and continues to revolve, around advocacy for the rights, power and status of women.

21st century: Gynocentrism continues

The now 800 year long culture of gynocentrism continues with the help of traditionalists eager to preserve gynocentric customs, manners, taboos, expectations, and institutions with which they have become so familiar; and also by feminists who continue to find new and often novel ways to increase women's power with the aid of chivalry. The modern feminist movement has rejected some chivalric customs such as opening car doors or giving up a seat on a bus for women; however they continue to rely on 'the spirit of chivalry' to attain new privileges for women: opening car doors has become opening doors into university or employment via affirmative action; and giving up seats on busses has become giving up seats in boardrooms and political parties via quotas. Despite the varied goals, contemporary gynocentrism remains a project for maintaining and increasing women's power with the assistance of chivalry.

Sources:

[1] Maurice Keen, *Chivalry*, Yale University Press, 1984. [Note: 1102 AD is the date ascribed to the writing of William's first poems].

[2] The dates 1168 – 1198 cover the period beginning with Eleanor and Marie's time at Poitiers to the time of Marie's death in 1198.
[3] Jeremy Catto, *Chivalry: The Path of Love*, Harper Collins, 1994.
[4] Jennifer G. Wollock, *Rethinking Chivalry and Courtly Love*, Praeger, 2011.

4. La Querelle des Femmes

The 800 year old *Querelle des Femmes* translates as the "quarrel about women" and amounts to what we today refer to as the "gender-war." In its narrow sense the term refers to a genre of Latin and French writing in which the superiority of one or the other sex has been proposed with the aim of determining the status of women.

In the broader sense, the *Querelle des Femmes* encompasses all writing in which the relative merits of the sexes are discussed with a gynocentric focus (*femmes*), sometimes using arguments and material drawn from the more narrowly defined literary debate. The centuries-long quarrel often revolved, and continues to revolve, around advocacy for the rights, power and status of women. If we consider the longevity of this revolution we might again be inclined to agree with Barbarosa's contention that feminism today is the tail end of "a perpetual advocacy machine for women".

The timeline of the *querelle* begins in the twelfth century, and after eight centuries of debate finds itself perpetuated in the feminist-driven reiterations of today (though some authors claim, unconvincingly, that the larger *querelle* came to an end in the 1700s).

For more about the history of *La Querelle des Femmes*, the following excerpt by historian Joan Kelly is instructive. Kelly's paper is written with a feminist focus thus leaving out all but the most superficial characterization of the male experience of gender relations. Nevertheless it provides much important history and for that I have no hesitation in quoting the introduction and encouraging the reader to gain a copy of the full essay if possible:

> "We generally think of feminism, and certainly of feminist theory, as taking rise in the nineteenth and twentieth centuries. Most histories of the Anglo-American women's movement acknowledge feminist "forerunners" in individual figures such as Anne Hutchinson, and in women inspired by the English and

French revolutions, but only with the women's rights conference at Seneca Falls in 1848 do they recognize the beginnings of a continuously developing body of feminist thought. Histories of French feminism claim a longer past. They tend to identify Christine de Pisan (1364-1430?) as the first to hold modern feminist views and then to survey other early figures who followed her in expressing prowoman ideas up until the time of the French Revolution.

New work is now appearing that will give us a fuller sense of the richness, coherence, and continuity of early feminist thought, and I hope this paper contributes to that end. What I hope to demonstrate is that there was a 400-year-old tradition of women thinking about women and sexual politics in European society *before* the French Revolution. Feminist theorizing arose in the fifteenth century, in intimate association with and in reaction to the new secular culture of the modern European state. It emerged as the voice of literate women who felt themselves and all women maligned and newly oppressed by that culture, but who were empowered by it at the same time to speak out in their defense. Christine de Pisan was the first such feminist thinker, and the four-century-long debate that she sparked, known as the *querelle des femmes*, became the vehicle through which most early feminist thinking evolved.

The early feminists did not use the term "feminist," of course. If they had applied any name to themselves, it would have been something like defenders or advocates of women, but it is fair to call this long line of prowomen writers that runs from Christine de Pisan to Mary Wollstonecraft by the name we use for their nineteenth- and twentieth-century descendants. Latter-day feminism, for all its additional richness, still incorporates the basic positions the feminists of the *querelle* were the first to take."[1]

Source:

[1] Joan Kelly, *Early Feminist Theory and the Querelle des Femmes* (1982)

5. Romance Writing as Medium

The sexual relations contract encoded in courtly love fiction was at first celebrated among the upper classes, but made its way by degrees eventually to the middle classes, and finally to the lower classes – or rather it broke class structure altogether in the sense that all Western peoples became inheritors of the customs of romantic love regardless of their social station.

Today the romantic novel is the biggest grossing genre of literature worldwide, with its themes saturating popular culture and its conventions informing politics and legislation globally.

The growth of this genre beyond the upper classes where it was born to become the lived story of all Western women is represented thematically here:

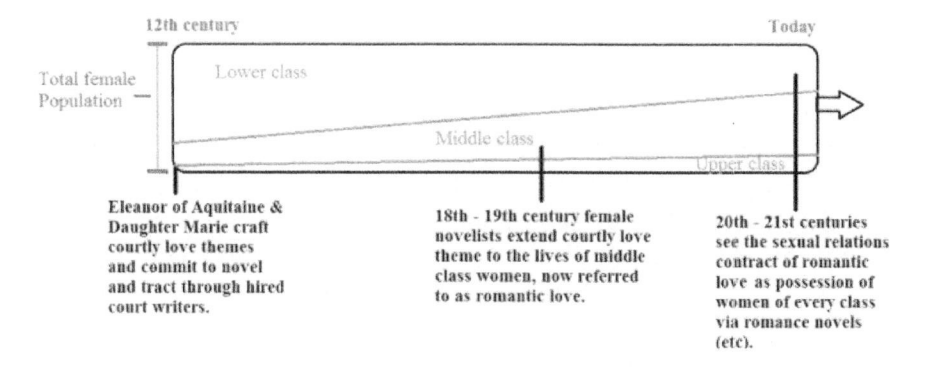

	12th century		Today
Total female Population	Lower class	Middle class	Upper class
	Eleanor of Aquitaine & Daughter Marie craft courtly love themes and commit to novel and tract through hired court writers.	18th - 19th century female novelists extend courtly love theme to the lives of middle class women, now referred to as romantic love.	20th - 21st centuries see the sexual relations contract of romantic love as possession of women of every class via romance novels (etc).

Upper-class beginnings

The three-stage evolution of romantic love saw its first chapter begin in 12th century France. Eleanor of Aquitaine and her daughter Marie De Champagne together elaborated the military notion of chivalry into a notion of servicing ladies, a practice otherwise known as 'courtly love.'

Courtly love was enacted by minstrels, playrights and troubadours, and especially via hired romance-writers like Chrétien de Troyes who wrote stories to illustrate its principles. Under the continuing guidance of Marie it was elaborated into a code of conduct by Andreas Capellanus in his famous tract titled 'About Love' (in English *The Art of Courtly Love*).

The aristocratic classes who developed this trope did not exist in a vacuum. The courtly themes they enacted would most certainly have captured the imaginations of the lower classes though public displays of pomp and pageantry, troubadours and tournaments, minstrels and playwrights, the telling of romantic stories, and of course the gossip flowing everywhere which would have exerted a powerful effect on the peasant imagination.

We cannot know for certain but it is likely that those of even lower classes adopted some assumptions portrayed in the public displays of courtly love, such as the importance of chivalrous behavior toward women and perhaps a belief in the Lady-like purity and moral superiority of women. Lucrezia Marinella provides just such an example of Venetian society from the year 1600:

> It is a marvelous sight in our city to see the wife of a shoemaker or butcher or even a porter all dressed up with gold chains round her neck, with pearls and valuable rings on her fingers, accompanied by a pair of women on either side to assist her and give her a hand, and then, by contrast, to see her husband cutting up meat all soiled with ox's blood and down at heel, or loaded up like a beast of burden dressed in rough cloth, as porters are.

> At first it may seem an astonishing anomaly to see the wife dressed like a lady and the husband so basely that he often appears to be her servant or butler, but if we consider the matter properly, we find it reasonable because it is necessary for a woman, even if she is humble and low, to be ornamented in this way because of her natural dignity and excellence, and for the man to be less so, like a servant or beast born to serve her.

Women have been honored by men with great and eminent titles that are used by them continually, being commonly referred to as *donne*, for the name donna means lady and mistress. When men refer to women thus, they honor them, though they may not intend to, by calling them ladies, even if they are humble and of a lowly disposition. In truth, to express the nobility of this sex men could not find a more appropriate and fitting name than *donna*, which immediately shows women's superiority and precedence over men, because by calling women mistress they show themselves of necessity to be subjects and servants.[1]

Middle class adaptation

The Victorian era saw the birth of mass novel writing, with much of it written by female authors. Whatever aspirations women had to romantic love in previous centuries, it was now actualized in writings by and about middle-class women, and the themes penned would become ritually enacted, ie. *lived*, by millions. This development is viewed by some researchers as marking a liberating revolution for middle class women.

Victorian peoples loved the traditional medieval romances of knights and ladies and they hoped to regain some of that noble, courtly behaviour and impress it upon the people both at home and in the wider empire. A new approach however saw it pitched beyond the upper classes to a larger group of people.

In her book *Male Masochism*, Carol Siegal[2] gives an overview of Victorian women's novels by focusing on the continuation and evolution of the romantic love themes found in medieval romances:

> "A great deal of what [Victorian] women's literary works had to say about gender relations may have been as disquieting as feminist political manifestos, and ironically so, in that the novels seem most anti-male in the very places where they most affirm a traditionally male vision of love. While women's lyric poetry tended to reverse the conventional gender roles in love by representing the female speaker as the lover instead of the

> object of love, women's fiction most frequently reproduced the images, so common in prior texts by men, of the self-abasing male lover and his exacting mistress. For example, in *Wuthering Heights*, Heathcliff declares himself Cathy's slave; in *Jane Eyre*, Rochester's desire for Jane is first inspired and then intensified by his physically dependent position; in *Middlemarch*, Will Ladislaw silently vows that Dorothea will always have him as her slave, his only claim to her love lies in how much he has suffered for her.
>
> In several Victorian novels by women, men must undergo quasi-ritualized humiliation or punishment before being judged deserving of their lady's attention. For instance, in Olive Schreiner's *Story of an African Farm*, the fair Lyndall condescends to treat her admirers tenderly after one has been horsewhipped and the other has dressed himself in women's clothes to wait on her. Although Victorian women's novels do explore the emotional insecurities of the heroines, their apparent *self-possession* is also stressed, in marked contrast to their lovers' displays of agony, desperation, and wounds."

Siegal suggests that male masochism and the dominatrix-like behavior of women in these writings is continuous with courtly love literature from the Middle Ages. And whilst some libertines self-consciously chose their lowly position in relation to women, the men described in Victorian women's novels *lacked* such volition:

> "These texts also insist that the true measure of male love is lack of volition. While the *heroines* make choices that define them morally, the heroes are helplessly compelled by love, and not judged to love unless they are helpless. In this respect Victorian women's fiction recovers the ethos so often expressed in medieval courtly romance that love must be "suffered as a destiny to be submitted to and not denied." It also departs from the conventions of medieval romance in describing the helpless submission to love as an attribute of true manliness, and thus Victorian women's fiction directly attacks the degeneration of chivalry into the self-conscious and controlled "gallantry" of eighteenth century libertines."

Those who have read medieval romance literature will a[gree with]
Siegal that the sexual relations contract embedded in Vi[ctorian]
Romance novels provides the continuation of a medieval [trope,]
not a fresh vision generally speaking. It is an example of

To be sure there are new elements in the Victorian novel, such as the stronger emphasis on emotion and the relaxing of class distinctions, but we are not dealing with a new animal in terms of larger trope structure, i.e. it is more like a new costume for an old play.

Said another way, the essence of the feudal relationship was *extracted* from the medieval class system in which it was born, and applied by authors of the Victorian era to people of the middle classes. With a passage of time and a further dissolving of class distinctions to which this trope might apply, it would be eventually applied to all people – class codes be damned.

The medieval structure in question is one we might call *sexual feudalism*. It is symbolized, for example, in the marriage proposal which sees men of any class go down on one knee – a ceremony originally intended for a feudal relationship contract in medieval times.

C.S. Lewis referred to the transfer of the feudal contract into intimate relations as "the feudalisation of love," making the observation that it has left no corner of our ethics, our imagination, or our daily life untouched. And perhaps more importantly this sexual feudalism – or romantic love as it is popularly called – no longer relies on a feudal society or class structures for its existence.

Taking an earnest look at the power wielded by protagonists in the Victorian woman's novel, and of the novel's real-world consequences for women, Nancy Armstrong[3] observes that the sexual contract can overrule the social contract, and that love can be the most powerful regulating law between two parties – a possibility that appears little considered by feminist writers.

Adaption by all levels of society

...ntic love today is the great leveler, smashing all class ...stinctions in its path. Women of low means can marry men of high station (and visa versa) because the love contract is capable of overruling the social contract. While there are literally millions of novels and movies that display feudalistic love overriding the social contract, the movie Pretty Woman, featuring Richard Gere and Julia Roberts, will suffice as a modern example:

> Edward Lewis, a successful corporate raider in Los Angeles on business, accidentally ends up on Hollywood Boulevard in the city's red-light district, after breaking up with his girlfriend during an unpleasant phone call. Leaving a party, he takes his lawyer's Lotus Esprit luxury car, and encounters a prostitute, Vivian Ward. He stops for her, having difficulties driving the car, and asks for directions to Beverly Hills. He asks her to get in and guide him to the Beverly Hills Regent Hotel, where he is staying. It becomes clear that Vivian knows more about the Lotus than he does, and he lets her drive. Vivian charges Lewis $20 for the ride, and they separate. She goes to a bus stop, where he finds her and offers to hire her for the night; later, he asks Vivian to play the role his girlfriend has refused, offering her $3000 to stay with him for the next six days as well as paying for a new, more acceptable wardrobe for her. That evening, visibly moved by her transformation, Edward begins seeing Vivian in a different light. He begins to open up to her, revealing his personal and business lives.
>
> Edward takes Vivian to a polo match in hopes of networking for his business deal. His attorney, Phillip, suspects Vivian is a corporate spy, and Edward tells him how they truly met. Phillip later approaches Vivian, suggesting they do business once her work with Edward is finished. Insulted, and furious that Edward has revealed their secret, Vivian wants to end the arrangement. Edward apologizes, and admits to feeling jealous of a business associate to whom Vivian paid attention at the match. Vivian's straightforward personality is rubbing off on Edward, and he finds himself acting in unaccustomed ways.

Clearly growing involved, Edward takes Vivian in his private jet to see La Traviata in San Francisco. Vivian is moved to tears by the story of the prostitute who falls in love with a rich man; after the opera, they appear to have fallen in love. Vivian breaks her "no kissing on the mouth" rule (which her friend Kit taught her), and he offers to put her up in an apartment so she can be off the streets. Hurt, she refuses, says this is not the "fairy tale" she dreamed of as a child, in which a knight on a white horse rescues her.

Meeting with the tycoon whose shipbuilding company he is in the process of "raiding," Edward changes his mind. His time with Vivian has shown him a different way of looking at life, and he suggests working together to save the company rather than tearing it apart and selling off the pieces. Phillip, furious at losing so much money, goes to the hotel to confront Edward, but finds only Vivian. Blaming her for the change in Edward, he attempts to rape her. Edward arrives, punches him in the face, and throws him out.

With his business in L.A. complete, Edward asks Vivian to stay one more night with him — because she wants to, not because he's paying her. She refuses. On his way to the airport, Edward re-thinks his life and has the hotel chauffeur detour to Vivian's apartment building, where he leaps from out the white limo's sun roof and "rescues her," an urban visual metaphor for the knight on a white horse of her dreams.[4]

The trope of romantic love is ubiquitous and pervasive through all levels of Westernized culture, and is rapidly infusing into remaining pockets of Asia that had been historically secluded from its influence. Romantic love is the number one selling genre in literature, movies and music globally – a testament to its all encompassing power.

The fact that women have been front-and-center in crafting and promoting this medieval "love" contract flies in the face of women's presumed powerless in the world. The two-spheres approach underlining powers unique to males and females is at play, and while only 1% of males traditionally controlled the political sphere, 100% of women possess the leverage of romantic love in the relational sphere. Further, I would go so far as to claim the political sphere governed by that 1% of men is now so captivated by the dictates of romantic love that its mission has become synonymous with the enactment of chivalry, both in social project spending, and in law.

The old saying is "Love conquers all." However the author of that phrase had in mind a very different kind of love from the all-conquering power we today refer to as romantic love, and women have played a pivotal role in bringing the later to bear.

Sources:

[1] Lucrezia Marinella, The Nobility and Excellence of Women and the Defects and Vices of Men (1600) Translated by Anne Dunhill, Published by University of Chicago Press
[2] Carol Siegal, *Male Masochism*, Indiana University Press, 1995 (pp. 12-13)
[3] Nancy Armstrong, *Desire and Domestic Fiction: A Political History of the Novel*, Oxford University Press, 1990
[4] Pretty Woman plot, from Wikipedia

Addendum:

I'm suspicious of scholarly works which "find" romantic love all over the world and in all periods. After reading many such essays I've come to the conclusion they confine themselves to biological universals such as the desire for sex, the need for attachment, limerence, social interaction and so on and so forth — all of which falls short of the complex European-derived phenomenon known as courtly & romantic love.

Those academic descriptions omit the idiosyncratic elements that might cast doubt on their universality thesis – details like male masochism, uniquely stylized feudal relationships from France or Germany, the conceptualization of the Virgin Mary and her purity and how that plays into conceptions of gender and love, along with other complex behaviors and influences which make up the courtly love complex arising in medieval Europe.

When Gaston Paris first coined the phrase 'Courtly Love' (1883) he was referring precisely to those idiosyncratic elements that render the phenomenon distinct from the universals many scholars reduce it to.

Gaston Paris' description of courtly love can be summarized as follows:

> "It is illicit, furtive and extra-conjugal; the lover continually fears lest he should, by some misfortune, displease his mistress or cease to be worthy of her; the male lover's position is one of inferiority; even the hardened warrior trembles in his lady's presence; she, on her part, makes her suitor acutely aware of his insecurity by deliberately acting in a capricious and haughty manner; love is a source of courage and refinement; the lady's apparent cruelty serves to test her lover's valor; finally, love, like chivalry and *courtoisie*, is an art with its own set of rules." [1]

Thus courtly love as defined by Paris has four distinctive traits;

> 1. It is illegitimate and furtive
> 2. The male lover is inferior and insecure; the beloved is elevated; haughty; even disdainful.
> 3. The lover must earn the lady's affection by undergoing tests of prowess, valor and devotion.
> 4. The love is an art and a science, subject to many rules and regulations — like courtesy in general.

It's clear that what we call romantic love today continues each of these conventions with the sole exception of *illegitimacy and furtiveness*. With this one exception romantic love can be regarded as coextensive with the courtly love described by Paris.

Many scholars researching this area conveniently overlook (or refuse to mention) the sexual feudalism inherent to the European-descended model of romantic love. Attempts to homogenise and cast romantic love as a global universal, while avoiding all mention of the unsavory sexual feudalism that might render it more problematic and complex, is unhelpful to say the least, and misleading at worst. European-descended romantic love, now the dominant version globally, deserves to be considered separately and need not be confused with more simple theoretical constructs on offer.

Note: [1] Roger Boase, *The Origin and Meaning of Courtly Love: A Critical Study of European Scholarship*, p.24, Manchester University Press, 1977

PART TWO

The Structure of Gynocentrism

6. Gynocentric Chivalry

Love and war have always been opposed, as we see in our usual phrase 'make love not war' or in the rhetoric of pro and anti-war camps. That the two are mutually exclusive is obvious enough. However, in twelfth century Europe something peculiar happened that ushered in a melding of these two contrary principles. Here the military code of chivalry was mated with the fancies of courtly love to produce a bastard child which we will here call *chivalric love* (today we simply label it 'chivalry'). Prior to this time chivalry always referred to the military code of behaviour –one that varied from country to country– but one which had absolutely nothing to do with romantic love.

What method did twelfth century society use to bring this about? In a word, *shaming*.

The medieval aristocracy began to ramp up the practice of shaming by choosing the worst behaviours of the most unruly males and extrapolating those behaviours to the entire gender. Sound familiar? Knights were particularly singled out –much like today's sporting heroes who display some kind of *faux pas*- to be used as examples of bad male behaviour requiring the remedy of sweeping cultural reform.

During this time of (supposedly) unruly males, uneducated squires were said to ride mangy horses into mess halls, and rude young men diverted eyes from psalters in the very midst of mass. Among the knights and in the atmosphere of tournaments occasional brawls with grisly incidents occurred – a cracked skull, a gouged eye – as the betting progressed and the dice flew. Male attention to clothing and fashion was said to be appalling, with men happy to go about in sheep and fox skins instead of clothes fashioned of rich and precious stuffs, in colours to better suit them in the company of ladies. And perhaps worst of all were their lack of refinement and manners toward women which was considered offensive.

How and by whom was this unruly gender going to be reformed? One of the first solutions was posed by a French Countess named Marie. According to historian Amy Kelly, with her male reforming ideas;

> "Marie organized the rabble of soldiers, fighting-cocks, jousters, springers, riding masters, troubadours, Poitevin nobles and debutantes, young chatelaines, adolescent princes, and infant princesses in the great hall of Poitiers. Of this pandemonium the countess fashioned a seemly and elegant society, the fame of which spread to the world. Here was a woman's assize to draw men from the excitements of the tilt and the hunt, from dice and games, to feminine society, an assize to outlaw boorishness and compel the tribute of adulation to female majesty."[1]

Countess Marie was one among a long line of reformers to help usher in a gynocentrism whose aim was to convince men of their shared flaws –essentially to shame them- and to prescribe romantic love and concomitant worship of females as the remedy. Via this program romantic love was welded onto the military code and introduced as a way to tame men's rowdiness and brutality, something today's traditionalists agree with in their call for men to adhere to these same male roles established first in medieval Europe. One of today's authorities on this period describes the training of knights in her observation, "The rise of courtly love and its intersection with chivalry in the West are both events of the twelfth century. The idea that love is ennobling and necessary for the education of a knight comes out of the lyrics of this period, but also in the romances of knighthood. Here the truest lovers are now the best knights."[2]

With romantic love firmly established within the chivalric code we begin to see the romantic behaviours of soldiers so familiar to us today; going to fight and die for his Lady, love letters from the front lines, a crumpled photo of his sweetheart in a uniform pocket. Rather than for man, king and country it is his love for "her" that now drives a man's military sacrifice. This is also the reason why today's movies portraying warzones and carnage always include a hero and his Lady/Damsel pausing for a passionate tongue kiss while the bombs explode around them, as if to suggest that all this carnage is for the sake of her and romantic love. Once accepted into the chivalric canon various love "rules" were enforced with military might –by white knights as we call them- and the resulting culture has been unstoppable. To try and stop it brings the wrath of all those white knights who will bury your ass into the ground for breaking this new military "goal" of romantic love.

Prior to the Middle Ages romantic love was usually considered with suspicion and even viewed as a sign of mental instability requiring removal from the source of trouble and perhaps a medical solution. In the context of universally arranged marriages, romantic love, if it was indulged at all, was done so in a discreet and often underground way without the sanction of polite society. This was the situation worldwide until the advent of the European revolution.

The cult of chivalric love took root first among the aristocratic classes and soon after reached the common classes through literature and storytelling. Romance literature in particular. Having germinated initially in Germany and France in the twelfth centuries, the cult spread on the wings of a burgeoning book production industry that would bring the gynocentric revolution to the entire European continent.

When one considers the subjects in these books – Gawain and Guinevere, Tristan and Isolde, heroic male deeds for women, love scandals, courtship, upper-class weddings, adultery, and status – we are reminded immediately of today's women's magazines that spill out of the magazine racks of shops and waiting rooms.

Women's magazines and the omnipresent romance novel –and women's gluttony for them- can be traced back to this early period in which the term *romance* was actually coined. According to Jennifer Wollock, a professor of Literature at Texas University, such literature had a substantial female readership along with mothers reading to their daughters. Wollock states that the continuing popularity of chivalric love stories is also confirmed by the provenance of romance manuscripts and contents of women's libraries of the late Middle Ages.[2]

The three behaviors of chivalric love-code

Keeping with the male side of the equation, the main behaviors prescribed by the code of chivalric love are the doing of romantic deeds, gallantry and vassalage.

Prior to its redeployment in romantic relationships *gallantry* referred to any courageous behaviour, especially in battle. The word can still mean that. However, under the rules of chivalric love it became, according to the Google dictionary definition, "Polite attention or respect given by men to women." Can these two definitions of gallantry be any further apart? Like the contraries of military chivalry vs. chivalric love, these two definitions of gallantry stretch the definition to cover two completely different domains of behaviour. It appears then that women of the time successfully harnessed men's greatest sacrificial behaviours –chivalry and gallantry- to indulge their narcissistic appetites.

A *vassal* is defined as a bondman, a slave, a subordinate or dependent, or a person who entered into a mutual obligation to a lord or monarch in the context of the feudal system in medieval Europe. The obligations often included military support and mutual protection in exchange for certain privileges, usually including the grant of land held as a fiefdom. Vassalage was then utilized as a conceit that Maurice Valency called "the shaping principle of the whole design of courtly love."[3] Whether it was a knight, troubadour, or commoner the vassal-to-woman routine was the order of the day then, exactly as it is today.[4] Poets adopted the terminology of feudalism, declaring themselves the vassal of the lady and addressing her as *midons* (my lord), which was taken as standard flattery of a woman. One particularly striking practice showing an adaption from the feudal model involved the man kneeling on one knee before the woman. By kneeling down in this way he assumes the posture of a vassal. He speaks, pledging his faith, promising, like a liege man, not to offer his services to anyone else. He goes even further: in the manner of a serf, he makes her a gift of his entire person.

Citing evidence of vassalism Amy Kelly writes, "As symbolized on shields and other illustrations that place the knight in the ritual attitude of commendation, kneeling before his lady with his hands folded between hers, homage signified male service, not domination or subordination of the lady, and it signified fidelity, constancy in that service."[5]

In short it was the lover's feudal relationship between vassal and overlord which provided the lover with a model for his humble and servile conduct.[2]

The lead actors – then and now

Imagine twelfth century Europe as a great stage performance enacting the themes of chivalric love, one that would become so popular its actors would continue to serve as role models for the global population 800 years later. The lead actors in this medieval play are as follows, accompanied (in brackets) with the titles we apply to those same actors today as they continue this ancient drama:

Courtly Ladies (= Feminists). Feminists today refer to courtly ladies of the late Middle Ages as the first feminists, or *protofeminists*, and as with modern feminists these women enjoyed considerable privilege and means. In the 12th – 14th centuries evidence shows that women began to agitate for increased authority over the 'correct' way for men and women to conduct relationships, with particular emphasis on what they felt were acceptable roles for males in a dignified and civil society. Not surprisingly this was precisely the time when powerful women were able to establish the female-headed 'courts of love' which acted in a comparable way to today's Family Courts in that both arbitrated love disputes between conflicting couples.

Key literature from the period detailing proper etiquette expected in gender relations was commissioned for writing by powerful women (eg. *The Art of Courtly love*) and in some cases was written by women themselves (eg. Christine de Pizan's writings or those of Marie de France). The emerging discourse acted like a drug that promised the introduction of a one-sided power for females over males, and through the dissemination of romance literature that promise rapidly spread to all social classes in the continent. We have been living with the consequences ever since, a revolution far more significant to the history gender relations than the introduction of the birth control pill and no-fault divorce combined- the latter being mere epiphenomena generated within a larger culture of chivalric love.

The archetypes introduced into society by these high-born ladies are instantly recognizable; the damsel in distress (women as innocent, woman as helpless, women as victim), the princess (women as beautiful, women as narcissistic subject requiring devotion, women as deserving of special privileges), and the high born Ladies (women as morally pure, women as precious, women as superior, women as entitled). These illusions ensured that the attentions of men would be spent attending to women, a program so successful that modern feminists continue to shape today's cultural landscape with the program of their protofeminists forebears. And just like their forebears, feminists continue to use shaming narratives to facilitate their pedestalizing inheritance.

White Knights (= White Knights). We retain this metaphor for such heroic individuals, men who are gallant in so many ways, but mostly the *wrong* ways such as showing-off to undeserving women and concomitantly delighting in competing with and hurting other men. More than any other player in this play, white knights specialize in gallant behaviour for the purpose of impressing and ultimately getting their egos stroked by women.

For these first white knights the tournament, the forerunner to modern sporting tournaments, consisted of chivalrous competitions or fights in the Middle Ages. In these fights knights were only too willing to hurt their fellow men to win the praise of female spectators. The competitors were observed doing battle by women who would throw their garments into the arena where the sportsmen would pick them up and wear pieces of women's clothes -hence the male wearing a particular woman's scarf would represent her in the tournament.

The men were basically fighting for "her" then, just as they did elsewhere on real battlefields for wife and mother. The gallant man who won his tournament was granted an opportunity to dally with the woman whom he represented in the ring. We retain this gynocentric tradition today as golf tournaments, football tournaments, martial arts tournaments and so on, all designed to show male prowess where the winning competitors get to dally with the best ladies.

Other activities of white knights include impressing women with big gestures of protection. For example, the 'Enterprise of the Green Shield with the White Lady' was a chivalric order founded by Jean Le Maingre and twelve knights in 1399 committing themselves to the protection of women. Inspired by the ideal of courtly love, the stated purpose of the order was to guard and defend the honour, estate, goods, reputation, fame and praise of all ladies and damsels, an undertaking that earned the praise of Christine de Pizan. Le Maingre, tired of receiving complaints from ladies, maidens, and widows claiming to be oppressed by powerful men bent on depriving them of the lands and honours, and finding no knight or squire willing to defend their just cause, founded an order of twelve knights sworn to carry "a shield of gold enamelled with green and a white lady inside".

The twelve knights, after swearing this oath, affirmed a long letter explaining their purpose and disseminated it widely in France and beyond her borders. The letter explained that any lady young or old finding herself the victim of injustice could petition one or more or the knights for redress and that knight would respond promptly and leave whatever other task he was performing to fight the lady's oppressor personally. The similarities of this Order with contemporary enterprises such as the White Ribbon Campaign in which male "ambassadors" pledge an oath to all of womanhood to never condone, excuse or remain silent about violence against women, and to intervene and take action against any man accused of wrongdoing against a woman. The similarities in these gallant missions make clear that the lineage of white knights has progressed seamlessly into the modern era.

Troubadours I (= "pick-up artistry" or "game" promoters). The troubadours' job was to spread the word about the virtues of chivalric love through music, song, poetry and storytelling. Aristocracy and commoner alike enjoyed hearing tales about bravery, and ladies were swept away with epic love poems as the troubadours practiced the rituals of chivalric love. Just like PUAs or Gamers today who write and speak in "praise of pussy," troubadours too were composers and promoters of the 'arts of love' aimed at securing sexual fulfilment.

Like those troubadours, Roosh and Roissy (etc.) continue the tradition of prose-writing to illustrate the many ways to flatter women in order to get into their pants. *Game* is a very apt word for this 800 yr old tradition, with its proscription for rehearsed lines and lack of personal authenticity. It is a scripted game of women-worship aimed at a narrow goal. In essence this Casanova routine amounts to a *feigning of chivalric love for the purposes of manipulation*, usually to gain sex. When modern women call these men 'players' they may be very close to the mark. While Roosh et.al. outwardly claim to reject chivalry, they nevertheless embrace its tenets like consummate thespians.

Troubadours II (= Profeminist Men – sometimes derogatorily named 'manginas'). Unlike the troubadours mentioned above who advocated for a love aimed at sexual fulfilment, Troubadour II advocated a more idealized love of longing that did not consummate in sexual fulfilment. In essence these men more resembled sycophantic Romeos than horny Casanovas. The guiding concept for them was called "fin' amors," which meant pure love. Such men were particularly prevalent in the north of France, whereas in the south we see that troubadours (type I mentioned up above) celebrated a love that was adulterous or carnal in which full sexual encounters were sought.

Another thing that distinguished type II troubadours from the former is authenticity. These men appeared to identify wholly with the role and were not merely players. The desire to serve women as their vassal, or perhaps as their masochistic slave, called upon their innermost character. Think of today's version being the typical profeminist men who work slavishly to pass on the message of their feminist superiors, much as these troubadours slaved to advocate the narcissistic idiosyncrasies of their Ladies. The vassalage role applies here more than with any other character of the Middle Ages – not as a merely pretentious means-to-an-end routine to gain sex, but rather as a soul-affirming act.

Which brings us to gynocentrism. It is clear from the foregoing that unless evidence of (broadspread) gynocentric culture can be found prior to the Middle Ages, then gynocentrism is precisely 800 years old. In order to determine if this thesis is valid we need first to define exactly what we mean by "gynocentrism".

The term gynocentrism has been in circulation since the 1800's, as far as I can tell, with the general definition being "focused on women; concerned with only women."[6] Adam Kostakis further qualifies gynocentrism as, "male sacrifice for the benefit of women" and "the deference of men to women," and he concludes; "Gynocentrism, whether it went by the name honor, nobility, chivalry, or feminism, its essence has gone unchanged. It remains a peculiarly male duty to help the women onto the lifeboats, while the men themselves face a certain and icy death."[7]

From these definitions we see that gynocentrism could refer to any one female-centered practice in an otherwise androcentric society, or to even a single gynocentric act carried out by one individual. With this broad usage in mind the phrase 'gynocentric culture' proves more precise for the purposes of this essay, which phrase I will define here as *any culture instituting rules for gender relationships that benefit females at the expense of males across a broad range of measures.*

At the base of our current form of gynocentrism lies the practice of enforced male sacrifice for the benefit of women. If we accept this definition we need to look back and ask the accompanying question of whether male sacrifices throughout history were always made for the sake of women, or alternatively for the sake of some other primary goal? For instance, when men went to die in vast numbers in wars, was it for women, or was it rather for Man, King and Country? If the latter we cannot then claim that this was a result of some intentional gynocentric culture, at least not in the way I have defined it here. If the sacrifice isn't intended for the benefit women, even if women were occasional beneficiaries of male sacrifice, then we are not dealing with gynocentrism.

Male disposability strictly "for the benefit of women" comes in strongly only after the advent of the 12th century gender revolution in Europe – a revolution that delivered us terms like gallantry, chivalry, chivalric love, courtesy, romance and so on. From that period onward gynocentric practices grew exponentially, culminating in the demands of today's feminism. In sum, gynocentrism was a patchy phenomenon at best before the middle ages, after which it became ubiquitous.

With all this in mind it makes little sense to talk of gynocentric culture starting with the industrial revolution a mere 200 years ago (or 100 or even 30 yrs ago), or of it being two million years old as some would argue. We are not simply fighting two million years of genetic programming; our culturally constructed enemy is much, *much* simpler to pinpoint and to potentially reverse. The historical evidence is strong. All we need do now is look at the circumstances under which gynocentrism first began to flourish and attempt to reverse those circumstances. Specifically, if gynocentric culture was brought about by the practice of shaming, then that is the enemy to target in order to reverse the entire enterprise. For me that process could begin by rejecting the fake moral purity to which women of the last millennia have pretended and against which the worst examples of men have been measured in order to shame the entire gender.

References

1. Amy Kelly, 'Eleanor of Aquitaine and Her Courts of Love' Source: Speculum, Vol. 12, No. 1 (Published by Medieval Academy of America, 1937)
2. Jennifer G. Wollock, Rethinking Chivalry and Courtly Love, (Published by Praeger, 2011)
3. Maurice Valency, In Praise of Love: An Introduction to the Love Poetry of the Renaissance, (Macmillan, 1961)
4. For an excellent article about vassaldom today see Gordon Wadsworth's 'The Western Butler and his Manhood' which indicates an unbroken line between the romantic vassaldom of the Middle Ages and the "butler" role expected of males today. (Published on AVfM, 2013)

5. Amy Kelly, 'Did Women Have a Renaissance?' in Women, History, and Theory (Published by UCP Press, 1984)
6. Dictionary.com – Gynocentric
7. Adam Kostakis, Gynocentrism Theory – (Published online, 2011). Although Kostakis assumes gynocentrism has been around throughout recorded history, he singles out the Middle Ages for comment: *"There is an enormous amount of continuity between the chivalric class code which arose in the Middle Ages and modern feminism... One could say that they are the same entity, which now exists in a more mature form – certainly, we are not dealing with two separate creatures."*

7. 'Frau Minne' the Goddess who steals men's hearts: a pictorial excursion

Above is a painting of *Frau Minne* from Southern Germany, 1320-1330 ca. The image depicts the lover presenting Frau Minne with his heart which has been pierced by three arrows. There are two German inscriptions with the image, the first of which translates as "Lady, send me solace, my heart has been wounded," while the second reads as "Gracious Lady, I have surrendered."

Frau Minne (*vrouw minne*) is the personification of courtly love from German Middle Ages. She is frequently addressed directly in Minnesang poetry, usually by a pining lover who is complaining about his state of suffering, but she also appears in the longer Minnerede poems, and in prose works.

She is often referred to as the "Goddess" of romantic love, which is differentiated strongly from other kinds of love such as Christian *agape* as embodied in the figure of Jesus. To make the distinction clear, romantic love is understood as *passion*, whereas Christian and Buddhist love is understood as *com*passion.

A rare allegorical painting of ca. 1400 (see figure 1), discovered in a guild house in Zurich in 2009 shows Frau Minne presiding over the suffering of male lovers who are having their hearts torn from their breasts. In this cruel scene Goddess Minne, the mistress of love, sits on a throne consisting of two men. She has just torn out the heart of a man to her left which she holds in her hand, while she is already cutting open the chest of another man to her right to rip his heart out.[1]

Figure 1: Goddess Minne sits on a throne made of two men, while proceeding to rip out the hearts of men in love

Romantic love involves the deployment of superstimuli, including titillating courtship rituals such as male chivalric servitude toward fetishized ladies that in many ways resembles the power dynamic of sado-masochistic practices. Such passion-inducing love contrasts with other kinds of love as mentioned above, such as friendship love, parental love extended to children, or that of Christianity or Buddhism which focuses on human compassion.

According to Johan Winkelman of the University of Amsterdam, *Frau Minne* is identified (see figure 2) with a crowned vulva carried aloft by servile, erect penises, thus depicting Minne by her most extreme elemental power.[2]

Figure 2: Badge displaying three phalli bearing a crowned vulva in a procession, 1375-1450, found in Brugge (Van Beuningen family collection, inventory number 652)

As mentioned in chapter five, romantic love began as a code of conduct among the aristocratic classes of the middle ages. However, the trend made its way by degrees eventually to the middle classes, and finally to the lower classes, and ultimately broke class distinctions altogether in the sense that all Western peoples became inheritors of the customs of romantic love regardless of their social station. This breaking of class barriers is marvellously rendered in the painting below by Hans Koberstein (figure 3), who portrays *Frau Minne* leading a helpless throng of individuals consisting of royalty and pauper, young and old, who are equally held under her sway.

Figure 3: *Frau Minne* smashes all class barriers, making rich and poor alike suffer from love sickness (Painting by Hans Koberstein, Germany, 1864-1945)

A 15th century depiction "The Power of Frau Minne" (figure 4) captures the pain and pathology so widely known to be part of the romantic love experience. The pathology associated with romantic love is so disturbing, in fact, that clinical psychologist Dr. Frank Tallis has written a book detailing the sickness associated with it based on his extensive clinical experience:

> Obsessive thoughts, erratic mood swings, insomnia, loss of appetite, recurrent and persistent images and impulses, superstitious or ritualistic compulsions, delusion, the inability to concentrate—exhibiting just five or six of these symptoms is enough to merit a diagnosis of a major depressive episode. Yet we all subconsciously welcome these symptoms when we allow ourselves to fall in love. In Love Sick, Dr. Frank Tallis, a leading authority on obsessive disorders, considers our experiences and expressions of love, and why the combinations of pleasure and pain, ecstasy and despair, rapture and grief have come to characterize what we mean when we speak of falling in love. Tallis examines why the agony associated with romantic love continues to be such a popular subject for poets, philosophers, songwriters, and scientists, and questions just how healthy our attitudes are and whether there may in fact be more sane, less tortured ways to love. A highly informative

exploration of how, throughout time, principally in the West, the symptoms of mental illness have been used to describe the state of being in love, this book offers an eloquent, thought-provoking, and endlessly illuminating look at one of the most important aspects of human behavior.[3]

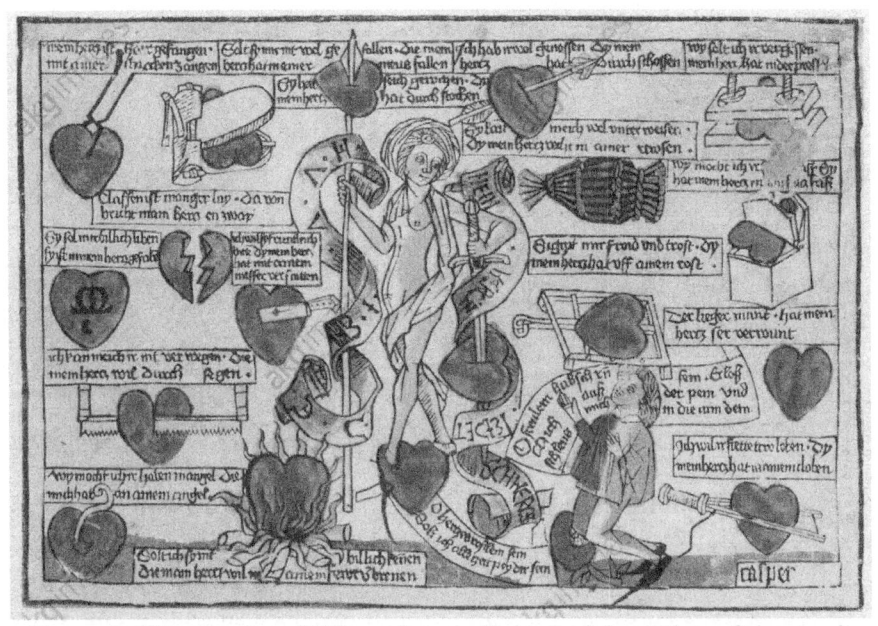

Figure 4: "The Power of Minne," - an allegorical depiction of women's power over men's hearts (Broadsheet woodcut, 15th century by Master Casper von Regensburg, Berlin, SMB, Kupferstichkabinett)

References:

[1] *Frau Minne hat sich gut gehalten*, 2009
[2] The world upside down. Secular badges and the iconography of the Late Medieval Period, in *Journal of Archaeology in the Low Countries 1-2 (November 2009)*
[3] *Love Sick: Love as a Mental Illness*, by Frank Tallis – overview on Goodreads

8. The sexual-relations contract

The gynocentric customs guiding relationships between the sexes originates in old Europe in the form of chivalry and courtly-love. The tradition began in 12th century France and Germany and spread rapidly to all the principle courts of Europe. From there it filtered into popular culture, being transported eventually to the new world on the wings of colonial expansionism – to the Americas, India, Australia and so on.

Why is this history important to men? Because it's a history we continue to enact today, unconsciously, and its consequences for men have far reaching psychological implications.

In the medieval model men offered themselves as vassals to women who took on the status of overlords in sexual relations – this because women were widely viewed as men's moral superiors. As evinced by the first troubadours, men pledged homage and fealty to women who actively played the part of man's superior. This feudalistic formula, which I will tentatively label sexual feudalism, is attested by writers from the Middle Ages onward, including by Lucrezia Marinella[1] who in 1600 AD recounted that women of even lower socioeconomic classes were treated as superiors by men who, she recounts, acted as servants or beasts born to serve them.

Many female and male writers stated this belief, including Modesta Pozzo who in 1590 wrote, "don't we see that men's rightful task is to go out to work and wear themselves out trying to accumulate wealth, as though they were our factors or stewards, so that we can remain at home like the lady of the house directing their work and enjoying the profit of their labors? That, if you like, is the reason why men are naturally stronger and more robust than us — they need to be, so they can put up with the hard labor they must endure in our service."[2]

And there is much more to this model than men laboring for women's material benefit. It also includes a belief in women's corporeal, moral and spiritual superiority, of which we shall say more below.

Sexual feudalism

I came to the phrase sexual feudalism as a shorthand for the sex-relations model of gynocentrism, and have since discovered the phrase used occasionally in literature; here are a few examples carrying the same meaning:

> Camille Paglia (1990):
>
> "…a sexual feudalism of master-slave relationships."
>
> Marjolijn Februari (2011):
>
> "Actually it's arguing for a dictatorship, the dictatorship of the vagina, a kind of sexual feudalism which you wouldn't want our international relations to be governed by in the future… those women aren't the least concerned about war and peace as a matter of principle; all they're concerned about is securing their own interests."
>
> Adam Kostakis (2011):
>
> "But what are the women's rights advocated today? The right to confiscate men's money, the right to commit parental alienation, the right to commit paternity fraud, the right to equal pay for less work, the right to pay a lower tax rate, the right to mutilate men, the right to confiscate sperm, the right to murder children, the right to not be disagreed with, the right to reproductive choice and the right to make that choice for men as well. In an interesting legal paradox, some have advocated – with success – that women should have the right to not be punished for crimes at all. The eventual outcome of this is a kind of sexual feudalism, where women rule arbitrarily, and men are held in bondage, with fewer rights and far more obligations."

When did it start?

Below are compiled a series of authoritative quotes on the subject. Each points to evidence of the beginnings of sexual feudalism in early Europe, along with other contributing factors such as veneration of the Virgin Mary and its influence on women's status.

■ H.J. Chaytor, The Troubadours[3]: "In the eleventh century the worship of the Virgin Mary became widely popular; the reverence bestowed upon the Virgin was extended to the female sex in general, and as a vassal owed obedience to his feudal overlord, so did he owe service and devotion to his lady… Thus there was a service of love as there was a service of vassalage, and the lover stood to his lady in a position analogous to that of the vassal to his overlord. He attained this position only by stages; "there are four stages in love: the first is that of aspirant (*fegnedor*), the second that of suppliant (*precador*), the third that of recognised suitor (*entendedor*) and the fourth that of accepted lover (*drut*)." The lover was formally installed as such by the lady, took an oath of fidelity to her and received a kiss to seal it, a ring or some other personal possession."

■ C.G. Crump, Legacy of the Middle Ages[4]: "The Aristocracy and Church developed the doctrine of the superiority of women, that adoration which gathered round both the persons both of the Virgin in heaven and the lady upon earth, and which handed down to the modern world the ideal of chivalry. The cult of the Virgin and the cult of chivalry grew together, and continually reacted upon one another… The cult of the lady was the mundane counterpart of the cult of the Virgin and it was the invention of the medieval aristocracy. In chivalry the romantic worship of a woman was as necessary a quality of the perfect knight as was the worship of God… It is obvious that the theory which regarded the worship of a lady as next to that of God and conceived of her as the mainspring of brave deeds, a creature half romantic, half divine, must have done something to counterbalance the dogma of subjection. The process of placing women upon a pedestal had begun, and whatever we may think of the ultimate value of such an elevation (for few human beings are suited to the part of stylites, whether ascetic or romantic) it was at least better than placing them, as the Fathers of the Church had inclined to do, in the bottomless pit."

- C.S. Lewis, The Allegory of Love[5]: "Everyone has heard of courtly love, and everyone knows it appeared quite suddenly at the end of the eleventh century at Languedoc. The sentiment, of course, is love, but love of a highly specialized sort, whose characteristics may be enumerated as Humility, Courtesy, and the Religion of Love. The lover is always abject. Obedience to his lady's lightest wish, however whimsical, and silent acquiescence in her rebukes, however unjust, are the only virtues he dares to claim. Here is a service of love closely modelled on the service which a feudal vassal owes to his lord. The lover is the lady's 'man'. He addresses her as *midons*, which etymologically represents not 'my lady' but 'my lord'. The whole attitude has been rightly described as 'a feudalisation of love'. This solemn amatory ritual is felt to be part and parcel of the courtly life."

- Joan Kelly, Did Women have a Renaissance?[6]: "Medieval courtly love, closely bound to the dominant values of feudalism and the Church, allowed in a special way for the expression of sexual love by women… if courtly love were to define itself as a noble phenomenon, it had to attribute an essential freedom to the relation between lovers. Hence, it metaphorically extended the social relation of vassalage to the love relationship, a "conceit" that Maurice Valency rightly called "the shaping principle of the whole design" of courtly love…

Thus, in Medieval romances, a parley typically followed a declaration of love until love freely proffered was freely returned. A kiss (like the kiss of homage) sealed the pledge, rings were exchanged, and the knight entered the love service of his lady. Representing love along the lines of vassalage had several liberating implications for aristocratic women. Most fundamental, ideas of homage and mutuality entered the notion of heterosexual relations along with the idea of freedom. As symbolized on shields and other illustrations that place the knight in the ritual attitude of commendation, kneeling before his lady with his hands folded between hers, homage signified male service, not domination or subordination of the lady, and it signified fidelity, constancy in that service."

- Peter Makin, Provence and Pound[7]: "William IX calls his lady *midons*, which I have translated as 'my Lord'. This midons is, as Pound said, 'inexplicable': it is used by the troubadours, of their ladies, and in the later troubadours we find it everywhere–Bernart de Ventadorn used it twenty-three times. Its etymology is (?*mi-*) dominus, 'my master, lord', but since it is used only of women – its pronoun is 'she' – glossarists have difficulty assigning it a gender. Though Mary Hackett has shown that it was not felt to mean on the *primary* level 'my quasi-feudal lord' by the troubadours who used it, these men knew their Latin and must have been aware of its origins and peculiarity; in fact it was clearly their collective emotions and expectations that drew what amounts to a metaphor from the area of lordship, just as it is the collective metaphor-making process that establishes 'baby' as a term for a girlfriend and that creates and transforms language constantly. In the same way, knowing that *Dominus* was the standard term for God, and that *don*, 'lord', was also used for God, they must also have felt some connection with religious adoration. William IX echoes the scriptures when he says;

> Every joy must bow down before her
> and every pride obey *Midons*…
> No one can find a finer lady,
> nor eyes see, nor mouth speak of…

The incantatory fifth stanza of this song enumerates powers that were evoked every day in the Virgin and the saints. William IX is, metaphorically, his lady's feudal vassal as well as her worshipper. So that there are three structures in parallel: the feudal, the courtly-love, and the religious; the psychological structure of each followed that of the others, so that it was difficult to think of any of them without transferring the feelings that belonged to the others. The lady was to lover as God to man, and as feudal lord to vassal; and feudal lord to vassal was as God to man. Our socio-economically minded age would say that the forms of feudal society must have shaped relationships in the other two spheres, and it is as likely that aesthetics and ethics moulded economics and vice versa. Of course, courtly love was not 'religious' in the sense of being part of any Christian ethic; it was a religion in its psychology. The courtly lover did not think of his lady as the Church thought of her, but as the Church thought of God."

■ Irving Singer, Love: Courtly and Romantic[8]: "Since the social structure of the Middle Ages was mainly feudal and hierarchical, men were expected to serve their lords while women were required to show fidelity. In courtly love this was transformed into meaning that the lover would serve his lady and that she would be faithful to him. Courtly love is often said to have placed women on a pedestal and to have made men into knights whose heroic lives would henceforth belong to elevated ladies. The idea arises from the fact that men frequently used the language of chivalry to express their servile relationship to whatever woman they loved, and sometimes they described her as a divinity toward which they might aspire but could never hope to equal… that he must prove himself worthy of her and so advance upward, step by step, toward a culminating union at her level; that everything noble and virtuous, everything that makes life worth living, proceeds from women, who are even described as the source of goodness itself. But though the lady now discourses with her lover, the men frequently cast themselves into the typical posture of fin'amors. On their knees, hands clasped, they beg the beloved to accept their love, their life, their service, and to do with them as she pleases."

■ Gerald A. Bond, A Handbook of the Troubadours[9]: "The extent of the penetration of feudal thought into the conception and expression of courtly love has been apparent to all modern investigators: the poet-lover portrays himself as a vassel (*om*), the lady is treated as a feudal lord and often addressed in masculine form (*midons/sidons*), and contracts (*conven*), reward (*guizardon*), and other aspects of loyal and humble service are constantly under discussion. In a profound sense, courtly love is quintessentially feudal (Riquer 77-96), for it imitates the primary hierarchical principles increasingly employed to control as well as to justify hegemonic desire in the second feudal age."

Sexual feudalism today

Despite occasional hand-wringing by the media about a decline in chivalric service to women, it appears to be alive and well. Not only are males continuing to go down on one knee to pop the question like good vassals, but sexual feudalism remains a popular staple of romance novels, Disney movies and cinematic blockbusters such as *Twilight*, and in popular music like Taylor Swift's *Love Story* which celebrates courtly love. Men are still willing to die, work, provide for, adore, and pedestalize women, and women are only too happy to be treated to such a dignifying display.

References:

[1] Lucrezia Marinella, *The Nobility and Excellence of Women and the Defects and Vices of Men* (1600)
[2] Modesta Pozzo, *The Worth of Women: their Nobility and Superiority to Men* (1590)
[3] H.J. Chaytor, *The Troubadours* (1913)
[4] C.G. Crump, *Legacy of the Middle Ages* (1943)
[5] C.S. Lewis, *The Allegory of Love* (1936)
[6] Joan Kelly, *Did Women have a Renaissance?* (1977)
[7] Peter Makin, *Provence and Pound* (1978)
[8] Irving Singer, *Love: Courtly and Romantic* (1984)
[9] Gerald A. Bond, *A Handbook of the Troubadours* (1995)

9. Damseling, Chivalry and Courtly Love

The dominant features of gender relations today come from old Europe in the forms of damseling, chivalry and courtly-love. Together they form the customs, in fact the *essence*, of modern gynocentric culture.

This holy trinity was crafted into a system of deportment by 12th century French and German aristocrats, setting a trend that spread to all the aristocratic courts of Europe. From those lofty parlors it filtered into popular culture, being transported eventually to the new world on the wings of colonial expansion.

The principle modes of transmission were expositions from upper class men and women; troubadour performances; plays; and notably a new genre of literature referred to as *romance literature* in which knights were celebrated for saving damsels in distress, and male lovers endured tortuous and trial-ridden tests in an attempt to secure a love bond with a beloved lady.

Nine hundred years later and romance novels remain the largest selling literature genre in the world, and we equally see the obsession with damseling and chivalry which dominate our politics, our societies, and our conversations over the dinner table.

In what follows, each of these gynocentric pillars and their historical roots will be summarized, along with references to the biological imperatives that give them their internal drive. Lastly (in *part 2*) an argument will be made that feminism today is nothing more, and nothing less, than a perpetuation of this medieval triad.

Let's take a closer look at these three elements.

Damseling

Damseling is a popular shorthand for women's projection of themselves as damsels in distress, regardless of whether the distress and the reasons for it are real or manufactured.

An excellent overview of damseling and its history was posted on Reddit in 2014 by author LemonMcAlister:

> We hear a lot about the "Damsel in Distress" trope and how it is both uncreative and damaging to women as a whole. The idea that a woman needs to be rescued by a valiant hero is held up as a sexist concept created by men who view women merely as a prize to be won.
>
> Would you be surprised if I told you this trope actually has a heavily feminist origin?
>
> In order to explain this, we'll need to go back in time about 1,000 years. In Medieval Europe, this was a time of rampant violence and wars with no other goal than material gain. Even long before the First Crusade, popular fiction took the form of heroic songs and epic poems much like Beowulf. They were sung in great halls and appealed mainly to a very masculine audience.

One thing many people are surprised to hear is that early legends and stories of King Arthur are exceedingly violent, gory, and action packed. Knights routinely have their head split to the shoulders, warriors are killed on almost every page, and there is even a giant who has his testicles sliced off in a fight.

The common understanding of Arthurian legend, however, is one of chivalry and courtly love. Knights fight for their ladies and for God. Love and romance is considered by most people to be a major part of the Arthurian stories.

The truth, however, is that this emphasis on love and romance, the idea that knights would fight to rescue a lady from a villain, is a later addition and was promoted by someone who can undeniably be called a feminist.

Eleanor of Aquitaine, born somewhere around 1123, was, as Wikipedia calls her, "one of the wealthiest and most powerful women in western Europe during the High Middle Ages". She is well known for doing many "unlady-like" things such as taking up the cross for the second crusade, recruiting women from her court to accompany her, and personally leading her own army as a feudal lord.

What's important here is that she is also responsible for the major and dramatic shift in the themes of popular fiction. Chrétien de Troyes, a poet of the late 12th century, is probably the most well-known writer dealing with this new type of Arthurian story. Some of these stories, in fact, were written for Eleanor's daughter, Marie de Champagne.

Emphasis was no longer placed on Arthur nor did these stories focus on a thoroughly manly knight's ability to split skulls. Arthur himself is used as a bit of a background decoration and is essentially a kindly old king that rules over his kingdom but doesn't take much of an active part in the stories.

The focus of the stories was on love, romance, and the concept that chivalry should emphasize a knight's utter devotion to his lady. Women also became more powerful. Far from being a prize to be won, they often helped their knights in one very important way or another.

In these stories, which are vastly different from earlier popular fiction, the love of a lady was the highest prize a knight could win, short of divine favor.

As society continued to change and we emerged from the dark ages, the stories remained immensely popular. There was no longer a need for savage and brutal warriors who could slaughter legions of people. Society's focus was on cultural ideals such as courtly love, romance, and the chivalric service of ladies.

My point here is that the original Arthurian stories, and essentially all popular fiction of the time, treated women as nothing more than a means to social, economic, and political advancement. The stories hardly ever included women and those that were present never played a significant role in the narrative.

It wasn't until Eleanor's reign, and the influence she had on popular fiction, that we see the development of the "Damsel in Distress" trope. This trope, however, was created because it appealed to women. It was an effort to include women in the enjoyment of popular fiction and marked a major change in society's values.

No longer were women merely an object, they were the entire motivation. No longer were they seen as merely a means to an end, they were the very focus of the story itself.

The "Damsel in Distress" trope is far from a misogynistic effort to treat women as prizes and is actually a result of the increased power and influence women were gaining during Eleanor's reign. It has continued to remain a popular story telling device because it appeals to both sexes by presenting an idealized view, both of society and what a hero's motivation should be.

The hero rescues the woman, placing himself in mortal danger, for love and love alone. Had we remained with the male dominated form of story-telling, the hero would rescue the damsel because marrying her would allow him to muster a larger army with which he could violently murder his chosen enemies. The woman's desire to be married to the hero would not factor into the equation at all.

Damsels are in distress because there is an extremely high value placed on them and they are, in many ways, the entire motivation for the hero and the story itself. The hero rescues the damsel because he is motivated by love, not by a desire to possess a prize.

The trials he goes through are tests not of his strength and masculinity but of his overpowering love for the damsel.

The damsel is, in other words, far more important than the hero.

As indicated in that summary, the chief goal of damseling is to evoke chivalric behaviors in men. The biological drive underpinning it is our urge to protect and provide for children, behavior which is triggered by juvenile characteristics such as a rounded forehead, large eyes, and most importantly *helplessness*.

As elaborated in a previous article, women have been taught from generation to generation to mimic juvenile characteristics via the use of makeup and vocal tonations, along with a feigning of distress typical of children — which collectively works to extract utility from men. While women are capable of solving most of their own problems and providing for their own needs and wants, many have cultivated a posture of helplessness, damseling their way out of doing the dirty, dangerous or stressful work required to achieve those goals.

Why exert yourself when men can be manipulated to do it for you?

Chivalry

Different definitions have been attached to the word chivalry throughout history. To make matters more confusing, encyclopedic overviews tend to blend those different meanings into an ungainly synthesis, making the job of teasing out distinctive meanings more difficult.

While there are differing definitions, the most common use of the term today is the one we need to describe. That job is made easy by modern dictionaries in which chivalry is given two separate and radically different definitions – a contemporary definition and an archaic, largely obsolete one:

> ▶ 1. very polite, honorable, and generous behaviour, especially by men towards women
> ▶ 2. the system of behaviour followed by knights in the medieval period of history, that put a high value on honour, knightly skill, and martial valor.[1]

The first is the definition we are concerned with here. To be sure, chivalry has been a woman-centered enterprise for close to a millennium, and early accounts such as that by Walter Scott in the year 1818 render the meaning clear:

> "The main ingredient in the spirit of Chivalry, second in force only to the religious zeal of its professors, and frequently predominating over it, was a devotion to the female sex, and particularly to her whom each knight selected as the chief object of his affection, of a nature so extravagant and unbounded as to approach to a sort of idolatry.
>
> "Amid the various duties of knighthood, that of protecting the female sex, respecting their persons, and redressing their wrongs, becoming the champion of their cause, and the chastiser of those by whom they were injured, was represented as one of the principal objects of the institution. Their oath

bound the new-made knights to defend the cause of all women without exception ; and the most pressing way of conjuring them to grant a boon was to implore it in the name of God and the ladies. The cause of a distressed lady was, in many instances, preferable to that even of the country to which the knight belonged.

"The defence of the female sex in general, the regard due to their honour, the subservience paid to their commands, the reverent awe and courtesy, which, in their presence, forbear all unseemly words and actions, were so blended with the institution of Chivalry as to form its very essence. But it was not enough that the "very perfect, gentle knight," should reverence the fair sex in general. It was essential to his character that he should select, as his proper choice, "a lady and a love," to be the polar star of his thoughts, the mistress of his affections, and the directress of his actions. In her service, he was to observe the duties of loyalty, faith, secrecy, and reverence.

Without such an empress of his heart, a knight, in the phrase of the times, was a ship without a rudder, a horse without a bridle, a sword without a hilt ; a being, in short, devoid of that ruling guidance and intelligence, which ought to inspire his bravery, and direct his actions.

Note the references to *protecting the female sex* and of *redressing their wrongs* as hallmarks of chivalry, with men going even so far as to believe the cause of a distressed lady is preferable to that of the nation to which he belonged.

But that protection, provision and adoration is only one half the story — the other half being fulfilled by the damsel in distress. The damsel represents the vulnerable and needy child who pulls on parental heartstrings, behavior provoking the parental brain state referred to by neurobiologists. Chivalry is shorthand for the parental brain state by which men are moved to protect, provide for and adore an adult disguised as a child.

Courtly love

Courtly love, which was later called romantic love, is the program of cultivating deference of men toward women. It was born as a twofold movement beginning with a social shaming of men for bad behaviors, followed by a proposal that men could atone for bad behavior by worship of women through a new code of love.

The idea was launched by powerful women of the medieval aristocracy who cited the worst behaviors of the most unruly males and extrapolated those behaviors to the entire gender. Knights were particularly singled out – much like today's sporting heroes who display some kind of faux pas – and used as examples of distasteful male behavior requiring the remedy of sweeping cultural reform.

During that time of (supposedly) unruly males, uneducated squires were said to ride mangy horses into mess halls, and rude young men diverted eyes from psalters in the very midst of mass. Among the knights and in the atmosphere of tournaments occasional brawls with grisly incidents occurred – a cracked skull, a gouged eye – as the betting progressed and the dice flew. Male attention to clothing and fashion was said to be appalling, with men happy to go about in sheep and fox skins instead of clothes fashioned of rich and precious stuffs, in colours to better suit them in the company of ladies. And perhaps worst of all were their lack of refinement and manners toward women which was considered reprehensible.

The solutions to the 'male problem' was posed by the French Countess Marie, daughter of Queen Eleanor of Aquitaine. Historian Amy Kelly tells;

> "Marie organized the rabble of soldiers, fighting-cocks, jousters, springers, riding masters, troubadours, Poitevin nobles and debutantes, young chatelaines, adolescent princes, and infant princesses in the great hall of Poitiers. Of this pandemonium the countess fashioned a seemly and elegant society, the fame of which spread to the world. Here was a woman's assize to draw men from the excitements of the tilt

and the hunt, from dice and games, to feminine society, an assize to outlaw boorishness and compel the tribute of adulation to female majesty."[2]

Marie was among the first of a long line of reformers to usher in a gynocentrism whose aim was to convince men of their shared flaws and to prescribe romantic love and concomitant worship of females as the remedy. The remedy was referred to as love service.

Love service involved the positioning of women as men's superiors along with a series of prescribed behaviors for demonstrating the sexual hierarchy in male-female interactions. The meta-rules for those interactions can be found in troubadour poetry and in the book *The Art of Courtly Love* by Andreas Capellanus, who wrote it under direction from Marie in 1188 AD.

The love service at the core of courtly love replicates feudal relations between vassals or serfs and their overlords. The feudal template was transferred wholesale into love relationships whereby each women came to be approached as a quasi 'lord' in each male-female relationship.

Sandra Alfonsi elaborated the feudalistic elements of courtly love in her book Masculine Submission in Troubadour Lyric:

> The troubadours lived and functioned within a society based on feudalism. Certain ones were themselves feudal lords; others were liegemen dependent on such lords for their sustinence. The troubadours who were members of the clergy were also actively involved in this feudal society. It is only natural that their literature reflect some traits of the age in which it was created. Scholars soon saw striking parallels between feudalistic practices and certain tenets of Courtly Love. The comparisons lie in certain resemblances shared by vassalage and the courtly "love service." Fundamental to both was the concept of obedience. As a vassal, the liegeman swore obedience to his lord. As a courtly lover, the poet chose a lady to whom he was required to swear obedience. Humility and obedience were two concepts familiar to medieval man, active

components of his Weltanschauung. Critics, such as Erich Kohler, have found them exhibited in both the life and literature of that time.

The entire concept of love-service was patterned after the vassal's oath to serve his lord with loyalty, tenacity, and courage. These same virtues were demanded of the poet. Like the liegeman vis-a-vis his sovereign, the poet approached his lady with fear and respect. Submitted to her, obedient to her will, he awaited a fief or honor as did the vassal. His compensation took many forms: the pleasure of his lady's company in her chamber or in the garden; an avowal of her love; a secret meeting; a kiss or even le surplus, complete unity. Like the lord, the woman who was venerated and served was expected to reward her faithful and humble servant.

The similarities between courtly service and vassalage are indeed striking. Although of a more refined character than an ordinary vassal, the poet-lover is portrayed as his lady's liegeman, involved in the ceremony of homage and pictured at the moment of the immixtio manuum. His reward for faithful service will doubtlessly include the osculum.

The influence of feudalism upon courtly love was, in my opinion, twofold: it provided the poets with a well-organized system of service after which they might pattern their own; it furnished them with a highly developed vocabulary centered around the service owed by a vassal to a lord. Feudalistic vocabulary was comprised of certain basic terminology indicative of the ties which legally bound a man to his lord in times of peace and war.[3]

Evolutionary Psychologist Don A. Monson paints a similar picture:

This configuration of unequal power is the central feature of the poet-lover's positioning of himself with regard to the love object. Drawing on the stratification and class-consciousness of medieval society, the canso describes primarily in terms of social hierarchy the woman's psycho-sexual power to determine the outcome of the relationship. Thus the troubadour's lady is regularly portrayed in terms denoting aristocracy, such as "noble" *rica, franca* or "high born" *de bon aire, de aut paratge*, whereas the poet stresses his own subordination, describing himself as "humble" *umil, umelian,* "submissive" *aclin*, and "obedient" *obedien*. The culmination of this tendency is one of the most pervasive images of troubadour poetry, the "feudal metaphor," which compares the relationship of the lover and his lady to that which obtains between a vassal and his lord.

The poet-lover presents himself to his lady in an attitude of feudal homage *omenatge*, "kneeling" *a/degenolhos* with "hands clasped" *mans jonchas*. He declares himself to be his lady's "man" *ome* or "liege man" *ome lige* and refers to the lady as his "lord" *senhor, midons*. He asks her to "retain" *retener* him as her "servant" *ser, servidor* or to take him into her "service" *servizi*. According to a military variant of the feudal metaphor, the lover "surrenders" *se rendre* to the lady, declaring himself "vanquished" *vencut* or "conquered" *conques*, and asks for her "mercy" *merce*.[4]

As described by Alfonsi and Monson, the demands of courtly love bespeak unbalanced power relationships, ones that engender vulnerability in the male supplicant along with an experience of a fragile pair-bonding that hovers in the realm of tantalizing.

In terms of our biological drives, courtly love captures the imperative for a strong, reliable pair-bonding experience, albeit one that remains maddeningly difficult to gain and maintain in the face of the convoluted conventions of courtly love.

The biological and cultural complexity covered above can be summarised in a few short lines;

Damseling is the cultural codification of neoteny.
Chivalry a cultural codification of the parental brain.
Courtly love is the codification of tantalizing pairbonds.

Part two of this series will look at how this holy trinity reappears in feminist ideology and activism.

References:

[1] Combination of Cambridge and Miriam-Webster dictionary definitions.
[2] Amy Kelly, *Eleanor of Aquitaine and Her Courts of Love*, Source: Speculum, Vol. 12, No. 1
[3] Sandra Alfonsi, *Masculine Submission in Troubadour Lyric*, 1986
[4] Don A. Monson, *Why is la Belle Dame sans Merci?*, Neophilologus 2011; 95: 523.

10. Taming Men for Women and State

Horses, dogs and men have one thing in common; they need training in order to shed their wild ways and become civilized. They need to be taught when to walk, run, sit, shit, play, work and, of course, when to cease fighting and attempting rape.

Women will do this for them.

From the pony club to the dog obedience class, and all the way through to wedding and relationship-advice magazines teaching "How to get him to do xyz," – women dominate the field of animal training.

Starting in childhood, girls are educated in the Pavlovian school[1] of human interactions, learning sexual manipulation, shaming and relational aggression as powerful techniques that if properly applied, will help transform men, and even the baddest of badboys, into proverbial Good Men.™ Is it any wonder then that when a woman sees a badboy she sees a creature with 'train me' written across his forehead, a task for which her whole life has been but a preparation….. a lady won't tolerate a feral animal wandering through the gynosphere, especially a handsome one, when she has the wherewithal to civilize him.

Let's take a little excursion through the history of taming.

Ancient Greece

Marriage is a particularly useful method by which men are tamed, so it's no surprise that the institution has been around for thousands of years. Hera, the Ancient Greek goddess of marriage was nicknamed 'The Tamer.' She tamed horses, men and heroes and in some places was recognized as the tamer of the seasons, of nature, or of the universe itself.

Hera's goal was to limit wildness and freedom by placing all creatures in service of civilized society. Her main tools-for-taming were the entrapment of men and women in marriage, the use of her own sexuality as an enticement for conformity, use of shaming language, and aggressive punishment of any rebellious behaviours – even for her lordly husband Zeus: "Hera's cruel rage tamed him."[2]

Hera was worshipped as 'Goddess of the yoke,' an enslaving device symbolizing her desire to make utilities out of beasts and men. She yoked obedient men to wives, and yoked male heroes to a performance of labours that bring betterment to women and society.

In the Iliad Hera is said to tame heroes through death, not marriage. Death through service to others was considered -and is still considered- something appropriate for males and for their own good. In *The Myth of Male Power* Warren Farrell recounts a Greek story which illustrates the problem:

The Hero As Slave:

Once upon a time, a mother who wanted to see the beautiful statue of Hera had no oxes or horses to carry her there. But she did have two sons. And the sons wanted more than anything to make their mother's wish come true. They volunteered to yoke themselves to a cart and take her over the mountains in the scorching heat to the faraway village of Argos, the home of the statue of Hera (the wife of Zeus). Upon their arrival in Argos, the sons were cheered and statues (that can be found to this day) were built in their honor. Their mother prayed that Hera give her sons the best gift in her power. Hera did that. The boys died. The traditional interpretation? The best thing that can happen to a man is to die at the height of his glory and power. Yet had this been a myth of two daughters who had substituted themselves for oxen to carry their father somewhere, would we have interpreted the daughters' deaths as proof that the best thing that can happen to a woman is to die at the height of her glory and power? The statues and cheers can be seen as bribes for the sons to value their lives less than their mother's request to view a statue. The fact that the statue was of Hera, the queen of the Olympian gods and protector of married women is symbolic. The sons' sacrifice symbolized the mandate for men to become strong enough to serve the needs of mothers and marriage, and to be willing to call it glory if they died in the process. Which is why the name Hercules means "for the glory of Hera".[3]

Yes these are myths, but on this topic life had a way of imitating art. Those who wrote the stories were drawing on experience to some extent, and married couples literally re-enacted the rituals of Hera and Zeus. In the marriage month (*Gamelion*) the mythical marriage of Hera and Zeus was reenacted and celebrated with public festivities, a time when many couples would get married in imitation of the divine couple. On these occasions prayers and offerings were given to Hera, and the bride would pledge fidelity to extending Hera's dominion on earth.

Women of Ancient Greece were considered, along with men, to be uncivilized and in need of taming for the greater good of society. Both sexes required a reconstruction in character and a submission to social responsibilities. Such was also the case in the Near East where an emerging Christian culture claimed that men and women were made of flawed stuff; women were born in original sin with Eve, sinful to the core, and were encouraged to aspire to the status of the holy and pure Virgin Mary. Likewise men were born in original sin and invited to improve their condition with *de imitatione Christi*, an imitation of Christ in order to bleach the stains from their imperfect souls.

While men and women in ancient times possessed equality in the depravity stakes, this was all to change in the Middle Ages.

Middle Ages

Fast forward to medieval times and we see a continuation of the desire to civilize human behaviour, except this time women are exempt from the taming to which the classical age subjected both sexes. By dint of a peculiar intersection of social beliefs, women came to be viewed as perfected from birth – due largely to the fact that worship of the Virgin Mary became amplified in the eleventh century and, by extension, the reverence bestowed upon the Virgin was extended to the female sex in general.[4] As Mary was perfect, so too became women.

No longer like the Biblical Eve striving to imitate the Mother of Christ, woman becomes Mary's counterpart on earth, and thus the cult of the "lady" is born as a mirror of the cult of the Virgin. Men for their part remain in the thoroughly fallen state of Adam while striving to imitate Jesus – knowing full well they will fall short of the goal. To enjoy the company of a lady a man must now prove himself worthy of her and so advance upward, step by step, toward a culminating union at her level; because everything noble and virtuous, everything that makes life worth living, proceeds from women, who are even described as the source of goodness itself.[5]

With the advent of women becoming men's moral superiors, it's here that men become the servants of women proper. It's here also that the *reciprocal* service previously entertained between the sexes begins its gradual decline in favour of gynocentrism. As the faithful owed obeisance to The Virgin, henceforth man must render his obeisance to the Virgin's earthly counterparts. Over the subsequent 100 years women even came to be viewed through the lens of the feudal contract whereby she became his overlord (*midons*), and he the vassal in dutiful service. It would be woman whose role it became to civilize the depraved, fallen creature called man by teaching him the gynocentric virtues of chivalry and courtly love.

Contemporary attitudes

Contemporary perspectives about civilizing males are divided between two superficially opposed camps – traditionalist women, and progressive feminists. I say superficially opposed because when the goals of both groups are compared they amount to exactly the same thing: the belief that morally superior women should enculturate men into the arts of chivalry and gentlemanliness for the benefit of women.

In a recent video promoting "A new kind of feminism for the 21st century," lifelong feminist and former National Organization for Women member, Tammy Bruce, articulated what she considers the time-honoured power of women; of being morally superior to men which includes the feminist responsibility of "civilizing" men's animalistic tendencies. She claims, "Women civilize men and it's what we're supposed to do. But in order to accomplish this critical task we must preserve our dignity, use the word 'no'…. that's the way to a new feminism, and the way to a better world for both sexes." [6]

Nothing new under the sun, hey?

Another feminist, Christina Hoff-Sommers agrees with this idea that men need to be civilized with chivalric manners, a belief she outlined in an interview with Emily Esfahani Smith, where she said, "Masculinity with morality and civility is a very powerful force for good. But masculinity without these virtues is dangerous—even lethal." "Chivalry is grounded in a fundamental reality that defines the relationship between the sexes," explained Sommers, "and given that most men are physically stronger than most women, men can overpower women at any time to get what they want." "If women give up on chivalry, it will be gone," continued Sommers. "If boys can get away with being boorish, they will, happily. Women will pay the price."[7]

Sommers elaborates her view in a 2009 interview with Ben Domenech:

> **Christina Hoff-Sommers:** Codes of gallantry and civility that developed over the centuries have served women very well. We badly need more of that male gallantry, but I hasten to say it's a reciprocal system. If males are going to be gallant then women also have a role to play. So today I think both sexes are remiss in nurturing this system.
>
> **Ben Domenech:** What in this era of post feminism that we live in today relationally would be the possible incentive for any man to be gallant when there doesn't seem to be any particular

reason that he has to be in order to function within today's relationship world?

Christina Hoff-Sommers: It's an interesting question because one of the things you find today is that most young men are gallant, and they are respectful, at least they are struggling to be. When I interview young men I ask them if they think it's a good thing to be a gentleman and almost all of them say yes; that word gentleman has a positive resonance with young men. Now, do they know how to be gentlemen, do they know what it entails? Many do not. And same with some young women, they are not necessarily behaving like ladies. So there's a lot of misunderstanding and lack of, perhaps, motivation. But it's still alive in people. I think still on a typical date a young man would pay for his date – it doesn't always happen in which case a girl would be resentful, and I can understand that…. These are gestures, I'm talking about certain gestures of respect – they need to be there and I think most women want them and I think men do too.

Ben Domenech: So why is that important? And I don't just mean that in the sense of continuing a relationship but in the larger sense of the term, and this is a frame that I have to ask you about: if the incentive there is a relationship that is going to lead to something, does it matter that the something is beyond the typical aspirations of today's men and women which seems to be more along the lines of a sex based relationship as opposed to one that actually has a longer term value beyond that prognosis.

Christina Hoff-Sommers: I think human beings at some point in their lives want something beyond a sex based relation. If you are going to build a relationship with someone it has been the case that women are going to be more likely to want to stay home and take care of the children, or certainly be more focused on that than the men, and I don't see that changing.

Ben Domenech: As a single dating male in today's environment there's a much lower bar that they have to clear, frankly, in order to bounce around the relationship scene with a good deal of happiness, at least in the temporary sense.

Christina Hoff-Sommers: Oh I have to agree, and I think in a way women sort of undid the social contract with men and released them from all the constraints. And we pay the price.[8]

For the sake of argument, and in order to demonstrate that progressive gynocentrism and traditionalist gynocentrism are both chasing male-only chivalry, here is a recent 'tradition-advocating' article by antifeminist Patrice Lewis that appears strikingly similar to the progressive model offered above by Bruce and Hoff-Sommers:

I admire men.

Specifically, I admire men who are controlled, confident and who fulfill their biological destiny as protectors and providers. Men are essential for training boys to tame the testosterone and channel their natural strengths and aggressiveness in appropriate ways. Trained men are, in the words of columnist Dennis Prager, the glory of civilization. (It goes without saying that untrained men are its scourge, but that's another column).

Men – trained, manly men – are necessary for a balanced society. They take on the tough ugly hard jobs women can't or won't do. They mine our coal and fight our fires and protect our shores and fix our engines and rescue our butts when we're in danger. They truck our goods and clean our pipes and wire our homes. They plow fields and grow food. They butcher livestock so we can buy meat in tidy sanitized packages in the grocery store and pretend it never came from a cow.

I'm not saying women can't be found in those fields; but let's be honest: The vast majority of workers in hard, dangerous, dirty and heavy fields are men. They deserve our praise and gratitude.

> Which is why I get so ticked off when feminists belittle men. These kinds of women don't admire manly men who protect and provide. Feminists don't want warriors; they want servants who will kowtow to their emotions and feeeeeeelings. They prefer emasculated androgynous guys who wouldn't know one end of a rifle from the other. Guys who watch chick flicks with them. Guys who know what temperature to wash the dainties. Guys who are preoccupied with "social justice" and bringing their carbon footprint down to zero.[9]

Lewis's argument above that boys are juicing with testosterone and need "taming" reveals an unbroken, and mythical conception of men stemming from ancient times – and it is wrong. Men are not born as wild animals in a testosterone-fuelled psychosis waiting to tear people from limb to limb. We need not buy our sons punching bags nor insert them into football training from 2 years of age to channel some androgen-fuelled chaos (doing it for fun, though, is another reason). The claim that men are unclean, bestial creatures in need of taming is not only false – it is extreme misandry and it needs to be challenged head on with each bigot who perpetuates it.

The above survey of man-taming by women spanning all the way from Ancient Greece, and through progressive feminism to regressive traditionalism, shows what we are up against. Nothing whatsoever has changed; chivalric servitude of men, trained into them by women (yes and by men), remains the order of the day. The one timeless voice echoing through all this is the monomyth of the animal-trainer – womankind and her pussy whip.

With the continuing encouragement of women to be dominatrix, and their enthusiasm to take on the role, is it any surprise that the majority of horse and dog training schools – obedience classes – are peopled by women? That so many little girls desire to possess their own pony is a no-brainer, and it's time we woke up to what this expensive little pastime symbolizes – the racing of horses may be the sport of Kings, but training of ponies is for the delight of princesses.

In a modern 'enlightened' society it's high time to ditch the idea that males, and only males, need taming. Let's instead rely on men's natural human empathy, a thing that exists in both sexes before the training begins. If you see a baby boy begin crying after he hears another baby crying nearby, it's a demonstration of empathy that is there from the start.[10] Like girls, boys develop mirror neurons which predispose them to be caring as they develop – we don't need to see them as heartless beasts in need of taming, curtailing or genitally maiming. So let's cease with the gynocentric boot-camp for males; they are already trained from the start by their own good natures – yes, men are good.

References:

[1] Anna Breslaw, The Pavlovian Blowjob –is it OK? (2012) (About sexual manipulation)
[2] Joan O'Brien, 'The Tamer of Heroes and Horses,' Chapter 6E in The Transformation of Hera, Rowman and Littlefield, (1993)
[3] Warren Farrell, The Myth of Male Power, Simon and Schuster, (1993)
[4] Peter Wright, The Sexual Relations Contract, Gynocentrism and its Cultural Origins
[5] Irving Singer, Love: Courtly and Romantic, UCP, 1984
[6] Tammy Bruce, Feminism 2.0, Prager University video (2014)
[7] Emily Esfahani Smith, 'Let's Give Chivalry Another Chance' The Atlantic, Dec 10 2012
[8] Interview with Christina Hoff-Sommers, "The Acculturated Podcast: Ladies and Gentlemen" 2009
[9] Patrice Lewis, 'Feminism Has Slain Our Protectors,' WND, 09/12/2014
[10] Daniel Goleman, Researchers Trace Empathy's Roots to Infancy, New York Times, 1989

11. Gynocentrism as a Narcissistic Pathology

Introduction

Gynocentrism has been described as a practice of prioritizing the needs, wants and desires of women over those of men. It operates within a moral hierarchy that emphasizes the innate *virtues* and *vulnerabilities* of women and the innate *vices* of men, thus providing a rationale for placing women's concerns and perspectives 'on top', and men's at the bottom (Nathanson & Young, 2006; 2010).

The same moral hierarchy has been institutionalized in social conventions, laws and interpretations of them, in constitutional amendments and their interpretive guidelines, and bureaucracies at every level of government, making gynocentrism de rigueur behind the scenes in law courts and government bureaucracies that result in systemic discrimination against men (Nathanson & Young, 2006; Wright, 2018a; Wallace et al., 2019; Naurin, 2019).

While gynocentric practices operate within most social institutions, they are equally observable within intimate heterosexual relationships in which men are expected to show deference to the needs, wants and desires of women, a practice referred to as chivalry or benevolent sexism (Wright, 2018b; Hammond et al., 2014; Naurin, et al., 2019).

In this article I set out to show that gynocentrism represents a gendered expression of narcissism, one that operates in the limited context of heterosexual relationships and exchanges.

To make a case that gynocentrism *is* narcissism we need first to define what narcissism is, which will be done by recounting the original Greek myth of Narcissus, followed by an overview of how the concept was taken up by the field of psychology and elaborated into a diagnostic entity. Next, this essay will take the diagnostic entity of narcissism and compare its formal criteria with those typically applied to the notion of gynocentrism to discover how closely, and in what ways, the two concepts align. Lastly the case will be made that narcissism, expressed as *gynocentricity,* is a delimited phenomenon depending on a gendered environment for its existence, and it thus qualifies as a form of 'situational narcissism' (Sherrill, 2001).

Narcissus myth

One day the handsome youth Narcissus became thirsty after a day hunting in the mountains with his companions. After discovering a pool of water he leaned upon its edge to drink and saw his face reflected in the water. Narcissus did not realize it was merely his own reflection and fell deeply in love with it, as if it was somebody else. Here is the account of his ordeal as told by Ovid:

> *While he seeks to slake his thirst another thirst springs up, and while he drinks he is smitten by the sight of the beautiful form he sees. He loves an unsubstantial hope and thinks that has substance which is only shadow. He looks in speechless wonder at himself and hangs there motionless in the same expression, like a statue carved from Parian marble. Prone on the ground, he gazes at his eyes, twin stars, and his locks, worthy of Bacchus, worthy of Apollo; on his smooth cheeks, his ivory neck, the glorious beauty of his face, the blush mingled*

with snowy white: all things, in short, he admires for which he is himself admired. Unwittingly he desires himself; he praises, and is himself what he praises; and while he seeks, is sought; equally he kindles love and burns with love. How often did he offer vain kisses on the elusive pool. How often did he plunge his arms into the water seeking to clasp the neck he sees there, but did not clasp himself in them!

What he sees he knows not; but that which he sees he burns for, and the same delusion mocks and allures his eyes. O fondly foolish boy, why vainly seek to clasp a fleeting image? What you seek is nowhere; but turn yourself away, and the object of your love will be no more. That which you behold is but the shadow of a reflected form and has no substance of its own. With you it comes, with you it stays, and it will go with you — if you can go.

No thought of food or rest can draw him from the spot; but, stretched on the shaded grass, he gazes on that false image with eyes that cannot look their fill and through his own eyes perishes. Raising himself a little, and stretching his arms to the trees, he cries:

"Did anyone, O ye woods, ever love more cruelly than I? You know, for you have been the convenient haunts of many lovers. Do you in the ages past, for your life is one of centuries, remember anyone who has pined away like this." I am charmed, and I see; but what I see and what charms me I cannot find — so great a delusion holds my love. And, to make me grieve the more, no mighty ocean separates us, no long road, no mountain ranges, no city walls with close-shut gates; by a thin barrier of water we are kept apart. He himself is eager to be embraced. For, often as I stretch my lips towards the lucent wave, so often with upturned face he strives to lift his lips to mine. You would think he could be touched — so small a thing it is that separates our loving hearts. Whoever you are, come forth hither! Why, O peerless youth, do you elude me? or whither do you go when I strive to reach you? Surely my form

and age are not such that you should shun them, and me too the nymphs have loved.

Some ground for hope you offer with your friendly looks, and when I have stretched out my arms to you, you stretch yours too. When I have smiled, you smile back; and I have often seen tears, when I weep, on your cheeks. My becks you answer with your nod; and, as I suspect from the movement of your sweet lips, you answer my words as well, but words which do not reach my ears. — Oh, I am he! I have felt it, I know now my own image, I burn with love of my own self; I both kindle the flames and suffer them. What shall I do. Shall I be wooed or woo. Why woo at all? What I desire, I have; the very abundance of my riches beggars me. Oh, that I might be parted from my own body! and, strange prayer for a lover, I would that what I love were absent from me! And now grief is sapping my strength; but a brief space of life remains to me and I am cut off in my life's prime. Death is nothing to me, for in death I shall leave my troubles; I would he that is loved might live longer; but as it is, we two shall die together in one breath."

He spoke and, half distraught, turned again to the same image. His tears ruffled the water, and dimly the image came back from the troubled pool. As he saw it thus depart, he cried: "Oh, whither do you flee? Stay here, and desert not him who loves thee, cruel one! Still may it be mine to gaze on what I may not touch, and by that gaze feed my unhappy passion." While he thus grieves, he plucks away his tunic at its upper fold and beats his bare breast with pallid hands. His breast when it is struck takes on a delicate glow; just as apples sometimes, though white in part, flush red in other part, or as grapes hanging in clusters take on a purple hue when not yet ripe. As soon as he sees this, when the water has become clear again, he can bear no more; but, as the yellow wax melts before a gentle heat, as hoar frost melts before the warm morning sun, so does he, wasted with love, pine away, and is slowly consumed by its hidden fire. (Ovid, 1916)

Unable to leave the allure of his own image, he came to realize that his love could not be reciprocated. Unable to eat, his body slowly wasted away from the fire of passion burning inside him, eventually disappearing entirely and transforming into a golden narcissus flower that still grows along the water's edge today.

Narcissism as a psychological designation

Twentieth century psychiatrists recognized the Narcissus myth as a useful metaphor for behaviors they were documenting in some of their patients, and so chose to refer to those behaviors as *narcissism*. As the primary symbol for representing narcissism was a male character, it may have helped to birth an assumption that narcissism is a mostly male pathology, which is misleading as both men and women can suffer from narcissistic excess. Early psychiatrists could equally have chosen a female character to symbolize the self-absorbed personality, such as the fairy-tale character Little Princess Cottongrass who, like Narcissus, became 'fixated with her own heart' while staring into a pool of water (Schwartz-Salant, 1982). '*Little Princess Cottongrass Personality Disorder,*' however, doesn't afford quite the same clinical gravitas.

The development of narcissism as a psychological concept has a long and complex history, covering ideas like *primary narcissism* (Freud, 1914) which is viewed as a healthy ingredient of childhood development, through to pathological manifestations that cause personal and interpersonal suffering, such as *narcissistic neurosis* (Freud, 1991) or *narcissistic personality disorder* (Campbell & Miller, 2011).

For the purpose of this study we will turn to the DSM-5 manual of psychological disorders which summarises narcissistic personality disorder as, *"a pervasive pattern of grandiosity (in fantasy or behavior), a constant need for admiration, and a lack of empathy."* (American Psychiatric Association, 2013, p. 670). The DSM's nine diagnostic criteria for narcissistic personality disorder will be detailed later, and compared point-by-point with gynocentric behaviors as described by relevant writers and scholars on the topic.

To begin with, we will touch on the concept of *acquired situational narcissism* as a qualifier of how gynocentric narcissism arises, contrasting it in this respect from narcissism that arises from developmental vicissitudes which resultin intractable personality disorder. While the diagnostic criteria for these narcissistic phenomena converge, their genesis is considerably different.

Acquired situational narcissism

Robert B Millman, Professor of Psychiatry at Cornell University, coined the phrase "acquired situational narcissism" (Plante, 2006). It refers to narcissistic behavior that is brought about or "triggered" by an experience of celebrity status, and manifests symptoms comparable to those listed for narcissistic personality disorder (Sherrill, 2001). Millman suggests that it is triggered by an experience of power that comes with any privileged occupational position or favoured social status. In this sense it is the environment that promotes the exaggeration of narcissistic traits in an individual which may have only existed previously as a mild trait or as latent potential.

Examples of acquired situational narcissism include *cultural narcissism* (Lasch, 2018; Twenge, 2006, 2009); *ingroup narcissism* (De Zavala, *et.al.*, 2009);*medical narcissism* (Banja, 2005); *celebrity narcissism* (Sherrill, 2001); and *leadership narcissism* (McSweeny, 2018). In this category we will include extreme gynocentricity displayed by women & girls as it manifests in the gendered context or 'situation' of interacting with men & boys (Wright, 2018b).

Gynocentrism

Before comparing gynocentric behaviours with the DSM-5 criteria for narcissistic personality disorder, we will need to isolate a consensual understanding of gynocentric behaviors from historical texts and modern theory. To that end we will start with three key historical texts, the first two from Lester F. Ward (1888, 1903) who was the first person to propose a general scientific theory of gynocentrism, and the second from Irish author George A. Birmingham;

Lester F. Ward:

"The female sex is primary in point both of origin and of importance in the history and economy of organic life. And as life is the highest product of nature, and human life the highest type of life, it follows that the grandest fact in nature is woman... Woman is the unchanging trunk of the great genealogic tree; while man, with all his vaunted superiority, is but a branch, a grafted scion, as it were, whose acquired qualities die with the individual, while those of woman are handed on to futurity. Woman is the race, and the race can be raised up only as she is raised up." (Ward, 1888)

"The gynæcocentric theory is the view that the female sex is primary and the male secondary in the organic scheme, that originally and normally all things center, as it were, about the female." (Ward, 1903)

George A. Birmingham:

"American social life seems to me — the word is one to apologize for — gynocentric. It is arranged with a view to the convenience and delight of women. Men come in where and how they can." (Birmingham, 1914)

In these pithy descriptions, gynocentrism defines women as both biological and social superiors in their relation to men who are positioned to support women's 'convenience and delight' where and how they can.

First wave feminist Charlotte Perkins-Gilman (1860 – 1935) claimed that the theory of gynocentrism was the most important contribution to 'the woman question' ever made (Gilman, 1911a; Davis, 2010). Commenting on Ward's gynæcocentric theory to doubters, she wrote

"You'll have to swallow it. The female is the race type; the male is her assistant. It is established beyond peradventure." (Gilman, 1911b, p.53). Perkins-Gilman's adherence to gynocentrism theory predated her introduction to Ward's theories, given in such poems as 'The Brood Mare' (Gillman, 1898) and others which she had written years before she met Ward. While continuing to laud Ward's gynocentrism theory as a brilliant contribution, she expanded on it by suggesting that women were more evolutionarily advanced than men, and that women were continuing to advance at a faster rate than men (Davis, 2010, p. 191).

More recently, American feminist Iris M. Young (1985) elaborated her gynocentric belief in a "superiority" of female values over male values, with the superiority thesis continuing to rest on a biological rationale as it did for Lester F. Ward and Perkins-Gilman above. Young states;

> *"Gynocentric feminism… argues for the superiority of the values embodied in traditionally female experience and rejects the values it finds in traditionally male dominated institutions… Gynocentric feminism finds in women's bodies and traditionally feminine activity the source of positive values. Women's reproductive processes keep us linked with nature and the promotion of life to a greater degree than men's. Female eroticism is more fluid, diffuse, and loving than violence-prone male sexuality. Our feminine socialization and traditional roles as mothers give us the capacity to nurture and a sense of social cooperation that may be the only salvation of the planet… within traditional femininity lie the values that we should promote for a better society."* (Young, 1985).

Note the biological essentialism appearing from Lester Ward through to Young who further states that *"Gynocentrism's most important contribution is its affirmation of difference"* (Young, 1985, p.184). Young clarifies that the superiority of "women's bodies" and the associated values of women's bodies are central tenets of both gynocentrism and third wave feminism, pointing to a biological essentialism that critics of feminism appear to have overlooked in their rush to denounce the social constructivism of some second-wave feminists (Wright, 2018c).

Since the 1970s most explorations of gynocentrism have been carried out by feminists from the perspective of what gynocentricity means to, or feels like, for women who embrace such behavior. They ask, for example, how does the practice of gynocentrism serve to strengthen women's ego-identity and improve their sense of dignity and wellbeing. Notably no equivalent discussion with men and boys has taken place to discover *their* experience of gynocentrism, thus the female-centric examination of the topic is an imbalanced one deserving of expansion by the inclusion of male, and also humanist perspectives in order to give a more complete overview of the topic.

Since the turn of the millennium new investigations into the nature and dynamics of gynocentrism – from male-inclusive, and humanist points of view – have appeared and provided a more detailed understanding of gynocentrism. The following examples present a synopsis of eight of these contributors: Alison Tieman, Paul Elam, Paul Nathanson & Katherine Young, Adam Kostakis, Peter wright, Dennis Gouws, and Peter Ryan.

> *Alison Tieman*
> "In my opinion – and this is just from observing the social systems as they play out – I would say that gynocentrism prioritizes women's protection and provision." (Elam & Tieman, 2018)
>
> *Paul Elam*
> "As gynocentrism manifests itself in the realm of sexual politics I do call it the tendency in human beings to prioritize the needs and wants of women over the needs and wants of men… The reason I like to frame it in terms of needs and wants is because in this gynocentric milieu, the gynocentric landscape in which we live, it's not just protection and provision that women demand of the culture around them, it is *everything*. Its protection, its provision, its privilege, its power, its 'believe the woman,' its, you know, if I say

something I don't want to be questioned; this goes way beyond protection and provision. (Elam & Tieman, 2018)

"How did chivalry go from being a military code to being a codified standard for men to meet in their protective treatment of women? The answer to that is a matter of historical record; it was through manipulation of the gynocentric instinct. In the twelfth century Eleanor of Aquitaine and her daughter Marie de Champagne engaged in an intensive campaign to popularize the idea of courtly or romantic love… Eleanor, a woman of serious means and influence, sort of like a supersized Betty Friedan of the high Middle Ages, saw an opportunity in this to promote a connection between men and women inspired by passion and infatuation and driven by a model of service – particularly of service to women. She and her daughter commissioned troubadours who borrowed from the ethics of military chivalry to write books and songs that carried this message to all the European courts. Even though the message was meant primarily for the aristocracy it eventually filtered down into the general population and quickly grew in popularity… The advent of romantic chivalrous love took the naturally occurring tendency in men to take care of women and made the first great leap toward a gynocentric society that would tolerate and indeed encourage all manner of insanity in the name of putting women first." (Elam,2016)

Paul Nathanson & Katherine Young
"In 'egalitarian' societies imagined by this branch of feminism, men were free to exist as "equals" of women as long as they acknowledged the supremacy of women. This worldview – as distinct from the one that produces objective scholarship on women – is explicitly gynocentric and therefore ignores the needs and problems of men.

Gynocentrism is a form of essentialism – as distinct from scholarship or political activity on behalf of women – to the extent that it focuses on the innate virtues of women. But this worldview is explicitly misandric too, because it not only ignores the needs and problems of men but also attacks men.

Misandry is a form of dualism that focuses on the innate vices of men. In this moral or even ontological hierarchy, women are at the top and men are at the bottom." (Nathanson & Young, 2010, p.58)

Adam Kostakis
"The traditional idea under discussion is male sacrifice for the benefit of women, which we term Gynocentrism. This is the historical norm, and it was the way of the world long before anything called 'feminism' made itself known. There is an enormous amount of continuity between the chivalric class code which arose in the Middle Ages and modern feminism, for instance. That the two are distinguishable is clear enough, but the latter is simply a progressive extension of the former over several centuries, having retained its essence over a long period of transition. One could say that they are the same entity, which now exists in a more mature form – certainly, we are not dealing with two separate creatures. (Kostakis, 2011a).

"And what is the logical outcome – say, if tomorrow, feminists got everything they are advocating for today? We would be plunged immediately into a two-tier system of rights and obligations, where men and women form distinct castes of citizen, the former weighed down by the obligations that enable the latter to luxuriate in their total autonomy. Life for women would be a literal lawlessness, while men's every move would be dictated from above, geared to the purpose of providing for all female needs and wants. It would not be inappropriate to call such a system sexual feudalism, and every time I read a feminist article, this is the impression that I get: that they aim to construct a new aristocracy, comprised only of women, while men stand at the gate, till in the fields, fight in their armies, and grovel at their feet for starvation wages. All feminist innovation and legislation creates new rights for women and new duties for men; thus it tends towards the creation of a male underclass. (Kostakis, 2011b).

"So, here is the definition I offer up: feminism is the most recent, and presently the most culturally dominant form of

Gynocentrism. It is a victim ideology which explicitly advocates female supremacy, at every facet of life in which men and women meet; it does so in accordance with its universalizing tendency, and so it does so in each sphere of life, including but extending beyond the political, social, cultural, personal, emotional, sexual, spiritual, economic, governmental and legal. By female supremacy, I refer to the notion that women should possess superiority of status, power and protection relative to men. It is the dominant cultural paradigm in the Western world and beyond. It is morally indefensible, although its adherents ensure that their hegemony goes unchallenged through the domination of societal institutions and the use of state violence." (Kostakis, 2011c).

Peter Wright
"Gynocentric chivalry is alluded to by alternative terms such as benevolent sexism, romantic love, gentlemanliness, courtesy, gallantry, heroism, or simply chivalry. The practice has roots in what some scholars have referred to as chivalric 'love service,' (Bennett, 2013) a ritualized form of devotion by men toward women popularized by troubadours in the Middle Ages. The earliest conceptualization of love service borrowed from the vocabulary of medieval feudalism, mimicking ties between a liegeman and his overlord; i.e., the male lover is referred to as *homo ligius* (the woman's liegeman, or 'my man') who pledged *honor*, and *servitium* (service) to the lady via a posture of feudal homage. The lady was addressed as *midons* (literally 'my lord'), and also by *dominus* (denoting the feudal Lady) (Alfonsi, 1986). These practices form the ideological taproot of modern romantic chivalry.

The conventions and indeed the lived practices of romantic chivalry celebrated first among the upper classes made their way by degrees eventually to the middle classes and finally to the lower classes – or rather they broke class structure altogether in the sense that all Western peoples became inheritors of the customs regardless of their social station. Today chivalry is a norm observed across the majority of global cultures, an explicitly gynocentric norm aimed to increase the comfort, safety and power of women, while affording men a sense of purpose and occasional heroism in addressing that same task.

C.S. Lewis referred to the growth of romantic chivalry as "the feudalisation of love," (Lewis, 2013, p. 2) making the observation that it has left no corner of our ethics, our imagination, or our daily life untouched. He observed that European society has moved essentially from a social feudalism, involving a contractual arrangement between a feudal lord and his vassal, to a sexual feudalism involving a comparable contract between men and women as symbolized in the act of a man going down on one knee to propose marriage. (Wright, 2018a)

"The dominant features of gender relations today come from old Europe in the forms of damseling, chivalry and courtly-love. Together they form the customs, in fact the essence, of modern gynocentric culture." (Wright, 2016)

Dennis Gouws
"This conservative approach to chivalry, one whose paternalism has surely outlived its usefulness in the twenty-first century, offers men little and confines them to a life of gynocentric pleasing and male disposability in the service of gynocentric chivalry. What this approach has in common with gender feminism is the way it suggests gynocentrism is essential and congruent with society—its natural and normal protocol—rather than being one philosophy among many. The second approach placed the onus on changing chivalry on women and their expectations. Ashley suggested that "It is women who need to figure out what roles they would have men perpetuate, and encourage those over the less-preferred actions." This approach completely objectifies men and empowers women to dictate what they want men to do to please women. It is gynocentric, strategic, and impersonal; it is a gender-feminist approach. As much of this chapter has suggested, it is harmful to men and women who seek gender equity.

"Michael Kimmel (Kalish & Kimmel, 2010) popularized the concept of aggrieved entitlement which can succinctly be defined as "a gendered emotion, a fusion of that humiliating loss of manhood and the moral obligation and entitlement to get it back" (p. 454). Because Kimmel's sympathies lie with gender feminism, he is uninterested in how this concept might apply to women's behavior. Women might express aggrieved entitlement when they experience what they perceive to be a humiliating loss of the gynocentric privilege to which gynocentric chivalry, gender feminism, and hegemonic gynarchy have entitled them. Self-righteous, angry expressions of personal offense and even violent acts might result from their perceived moral obligation to regain their sense of gynocentric privilege. A cursory internet search of gender-feminist responses to men's-issues speakers on campus and to the establishing men's groups or other male-positive spaces on campus will provide examples of this aggrieved entitlement." (Gouws, 2018)

Peter Ryan
I define gynocentrism as the following: The set of elements of society and relationships that are directed by the intent to prioritise female well-being over male well-being, based solely or partly on the sex of the intended beneficiary(ies) being female and for which there are no equivalent efforts made to provide corresponding commensurate benefits to males.

I define well-being as the quality of the overall condition of the life of an individual or group, that is based on taking their mental and physical health and life satisfaction into consideration.

The diagnostic criteria that must be met for an element of society or relationships to be considered gynocentric are the following: 1. The element must be driven by the intent to prioritise female well-being over male well-being. 2. This intent must be solely or partly based on the sex of the intended beneficiary(ies) being female. 3. There must be no equivalent efforts made to provide commensurate benefits to males for instances where female well-being is prioritised over male well-being." (Ryan, 2018)

Online reference definitions

"**Gynocentrism:** Is a radical feminist discourse that champions woman-centered beliefs, identities, and social organization." (Encyclopedia R., 2005)

"**Gynocentric:** Centered on or concerned exclusively with women; taking a female (or specifically a feminist) point of view." (Dictionary, O. E., 2008)

"**Gynocentrism:** The tendency to place the female or feminine viewpoint and experience at the center of a society or culture." (Dictionary S. D., 2016)

"**Gynocentrism:** An ideological focus on females, and issues affecting them, possibly to the detriment of non-females." (Dictionary, Y., 2018)

"**Gynocentrism:** Dominated by or emphasizing feminine interests or a feminine point of view." (Dictionary, M. W., 2020)

Condensation and summary of descriptions of gynocentrism:

1. By definition males and females in gynocentric relationships are both ideologically and behaviourally 'woman-centered' as per the suffix *-centrism*. In this respect gynocentrism is differentiated from relationships that are *relationship-centered*, involving reciprocity between men and women, relationship partners, and other family members.

2. Gynocentric relationships assume strict gender roles: men are expected to pedestalize and extend chivalric (benevolently sexist) behavior toward women; and women are to assume the status of biological and moral superiority deserving of pedestalization and entitlement to special benefits. These roles have roots in the tradition of courtly and romantic love.

3. Gynocentrism is focused on maximizing the benefits of convenience, comfort, pleasure, needs, wants, protections, provision, power and self-esteem of women.

4. It takes place in heterosexual relationships, or by extension in relationships where stereotypical heterosexual roles can be mimicked. In this sense it is situational (heterosexual relationships) rather than universal and general.

5. It obliterates the variety of potential masculinities, and replaces them with the singular masculinity of chivalric servant. Masculine variety of every non-gynocentric kind is viewed as a failure and affront to the gynocentric mandate.

DSM criteria for Narcissistic Personality Disorder

The DSM-5 states that narcissistic personality disorder is indicated by the presence of at least 5 of 9 criteria (See table-1 below). For the purpose of this study, the DSM criteria are compared below with behaviors typically inferred of the 'gynocentric woman' [GW].

TABLE - 1

DSM-5 diagnostic criteria for Narcissistic Personality Disorder	Traits and behaviors of the gynocentrism-oriented woman

[DSM] 1. A grandiose sense of self-importance (eg, the individual exaggerates achievements and talents and expects to be recognized as superior without commensurate achievements)	[GW] Views self as 'superior' to males (e.g. genetically, physically, morally, creatively, aesthetically, or in terms of emotional intelligence) based on the fact of being born female (Ward, 1903; Young, 1985)
[DSM] 2. A preoccupation with fantasies of unlimited success, power, brilliance, beauty, or ideal love	[GW] Preoccupied with fantasies of unlimited success, power, brilliance, beauty, or ideal love, appearing especially in the gendered context of the romantic love tradition (Wright, 2014)
[DSM] 3. A belief that he or she is special and unique and can only be understood by, or should associate with, other special or high-status people or institutions	[GW] Gynocentric feminists have long celebrated women's special and unique "ways of knowing," along with the mystical association women share through these paths (Belenky, et al., 1986; Gilligan, 1993)
[DSM] 4. A need for excessive admiration	[GW] Expects men to pedestalize herself and/or women generally. Pedestalization is defined by some authors as a central defining feature of gynocentrism. (Galbi, 2015; Jarosek, 2017)
[DSM] 5. A sense of entitlement (ie, unreasonable expectations of especially favorable treatment or automatic compliance with his or her expectations)	[GW] Feels entitled to receive gestures of benevolent sexism/chivalry, and deferential behavior from intimate and familial males (Hammond, et al., 2014; Wright, 2018b)

[DSM] 6. Interpersonally exploitive behavior (ie, the individual takes advantage of others to achieve his or her own ends)	[GW] Pressures, manipulates or demands to receive benevolently sexist gestures from men in order to secure comforts, pleasures, needs, wants, protections, provision, power and self-esteem. Employs intimidating or punishing gestures for failures and non-compliance (Wright, 2018b; 2019)
[DSM] 7. A lack of empathy (unwillingness to recognize or identify with the feelings and needs of others)	[GW] Supresses, ignores or actively censures empathic responses to men's issues. This approach is promoted by gynocentric feminists who treat dispensation of empathy as a zero-sum activity and scarce resource that must be reserved exclusively for women(Collins, 2016; Fiamengo, 2015)
[DSM] 8. Envy of others or a belief that others are envious of him or her	[GW] Envious of other women's beauty, or assumes others envious of her beauty; viewed as a competitive edge for securing male resources and admiration. (Friday, 1996) Also demonstrates envy and concomitant resentment of male potency and provision (Schoenewolf, 2017; Reich,1953)
[DSM] 9. A demonstration of arrogant and haughty behaviors or attitudes	[GW] Displays an attitude and behavior of superiority over, and concomitant contempt for, men and boys. (Kostakis, 2011c; Nathanson & Young, 2001; Schoenewolf, 2017)

Related theories of narcissism

The lexicon of narcissism-related terms provides further items that can be explored to determine the degree to which gynocentrism reflects narcissistic behaviors. Three topics are surveyed below to help to inform the current study.

'Narcissistic supply' is a concept introduced into psychoanalytic theory by Otto Fenichel (1938) to describe a type of admiration, interpersonal support or sustenance drawn by an individual from his or her environment that is essential to the formation of self-esteem. The individual employs two main strategies for eliciting narcissistic supplies from others; ingratiation and aggression. While Fenichel referred to the need for narcissistic supply as a human universal, he underlined its potential to develop into exaggerated and pathological forms (Fenichel, 1938). The phrase is typically employed in the pathological sense, describing an excessive need for attention or admiration and operating as a form of interpersonal exploitation in which the narcissist fails to take into account the wider feelings, opinions, or needs of other people.

Self-psychologist Heinz Kohut believed individuals with narcissistic personality disorder experience a mental disintegration when cut off from a regular source of narcissistic supply. Those providing supplies are sometimes treated as if they are a part of the narcissist in an eclipse of all personal boundaries (Kohut & Tolpin, 1996). The same motivations and behaviors are readily seen in the gynocentrically-oriented women's search for, and expectation of receiving, chivalric supplies from men (Hammond et al., 2014; Wright, 2018b).

'Narcissistic injury' refers is a psychological wounding of the self through lack of narcissistic supplies. It can arise from absence of a supplying audience, or alternatively by their refusal or failure to offer adequate ego support. Such a blow typically lowers the narcissist's self-esteem and produces feelings of humiliation, shame and rage (Reber, 1995).

In the marketplace of potential narcissistic supplies, women are frequently afforded priority over men, culturally speaking, such as we witness in phrases like "The wedding is *her* special day," "Ladies before gentlemen," "Aint nobody happy if mamma ain't happy," "Women and girls first," "Whatever she wants, she gets," "Men must pay the bill for dinner," etc. When denied the experience of gynocentric entitlements women may experience narcissistic injury, and may express a sense of aggrieved entitlement (Gouws, 2018; Wright, 2019).

'*Narcissistic rage*' refers to an aggressive reaction arising from the experience of a narcissistic injury that has threatened the narcissist's self-esteem or self-worth. The intensity of the reaction occurs on a continuum, which may range from instances of aloofness and expressions of mild irritation or annoyance, to serious outbursts including, at the extremes, violent attacks or homicide (Lambe, et al., 2018).

For Heinz Kohut, narcissistic rage is related to narcissists' need for total control of their environment, including "the need for revenge, for righting a wrong, for undoing a hurt by whatever means." (Ronningstam, 2005, pp. 86–87). It is an attempt by the narcissist to turn a passive experience of victimization into an active role via giving pain to others, while at the same time attempting to rebuild some sense of self-worth. It may also involve self-preservation, with rage serving to restore a sense of safety and power by destroying that which had threatened the narcissist.(Ronningstam, 2005). Edmund Bergler states that the rage follows any blow to the narcissist's sense of omnipotence (Levin, 1995).

Viewed within the context of gynocentric relationships, narcissistic rage, or what we might loosely term *gynocentric rage*, is captured in the phrase "Hell hath no fury like a woman scorned," which indicates that a woman who cannot make someone love her can become extremely angry and vindictive (Gouws, 2018; Wright, 2019).

Discussion

Benevolent sexism (chivalry) plays a significant role in the operation and maintenance of gynocentric relationships, and warrants further analysis in the context of this study.

In their paper titled *The Allure of Sexism*, Matthew D Hammond *et.al.* studied whether women's feeling of entitlement to special treatment, which they emphasize is "a central facet of narcissism based on feelings of superiority and deservingness" (2014, p.422), was linked with endorsement of benevolent sexism by women across time. Perhaps unsurprisingly, the study found that a psychological sense of entitlement by women *does* mediate endorsement of benevolent sexism. Moreover, the researchers theorized that characteristics of narcissistic entitlement, those which drive resource-attainment and self-enhancement strategies, are the same qualities that promote women's adoption of benevolent sexism:

> *"First, benevolent sexism facilitates the capacity to gain material resources and complements feelings of deservingness by promoting a structure of intimate relationships in which men use their access to social power and status to provide for women (Chen et al., 2009). Second, benevolent sexism reinforces beliefs of superiority by expressing praise and reverence of women, emphasizing qualities of purity, morality, and culture which make women the "fairer sex." Indeed, identifying with these kinds of gender-related beliefs (e.g., women are warm) fosters a more positive self-concept (Rudman, Greenwald, & McGhee, 2001).*
>
> *Moreover, for women higher in psychological entitlement, benevolent sexism legitimizes a self-centric approach to relationships by emphasizing women's special status within the intimate domain and men's responsibilities of providing and caring for women. Such care involves everyday chivalrous behaviors, such as paying on a first date and opening doors for women (Sarlet et al., 2012; Viki et al., 2003), to more overarching prescriptions for men's behavior toward women, such as being "willing to sacrifice their own well-being" to provide for women and to ensure women's happiness by placing her "on a pedestal" (Ambivalent Sexism Inventory;*

Glick & Fiske, 1996). Thus, women higher in psychological entitlement should be particularly enticed by benevolent sexism because it justifies provision and praise from men as expected behavior and does not require women to reciprocate the reverence or material gains, which men provide.' (Hammond, et al., 2014, pp. 3-4).

Recognition of narcissism as prevalent among feminist women has a long history. In her paper *Who Put The "Me" in Feminism,* Imogen Tyler (2005) admits to the widespread recognition of narcissism in the feminist movement by wider society. Tyler attempts to put a positive spin on the behavior, reframing the predilection among feminists as a result of downtrodden women's attempt to develop an independent, healthy narcissistic identity not tied to oppressive patriarchal demands. Tyler further advocates what she views as the hidden benefits of female narcissism:

> *"Feminism exposes and challenges the sexual politics of narcissism both by making prevailing forms of narcissism visible (the homo-social bond) and by encouraging new self-conscious forms of narcissism amongst women to emerge."*
>
> *"In this article I have examined what is at stake in the attribution of narcissism to femininity and feminism, and the routes through which arguments about 'feminist narcissism' became central to the popular abjection of feminism… Despite the ways in which narcissism has been consistently employed as a rhetorical means of denigrating women and delegitimizing feminist politics, I have also demonstrated the central role of narcissistic theories of identity in enabling feminist theorists to prise open the mechanisms of feminine identity and critique the sexual politics of identity practices."* (Tyler, 2005)

The narcissistic individual's sense of entitlement, combined with an unwillingness to identify with the feelings and needs of relationship partners, renders their relationships decidedly narcissist-centered. The relationship partner is objectified as a "thing," a resource provider who is pressured to follow the narcissist's lead, or alternatively to suffer punishment, rejection or dissolution of the relationship.

Likewise, highly gynocentric relationships center around needs and wants of women, with the male partner expected to assist in serving those aims in place of his own. Writer C.S. Lewis captured this dynamic in his description of courtly love, where he elaborated male lover's posture in relation to his lady; *"The lover is always abject. Obedience to his lady's lightest wish, however whimsical, and silent acquiescence in her rebukes, however unjust, are the only virtues he dares to claim."* (Lewis, 2013, p. 2). These findings are suggested in the term gynocentrism itself whose suffix *–centrism–* emphasizes dominance of the female position over inclusivity, compromise, and power-sharing relationships. Said alternatively, couple-centeredness and gyno-centeredness (woman centeredness) are antithetical concepts.

A note on terminology needs to be made at this juncture. The phrase "Gynocentric relationships," as used throughout this study, is differentiated by the author from all isolated gynocentric acts, such as an annual celebration of Mother's Day. Or for a more dramatic illustration of an isolated gynocentric act, we might picture a man taking on a knife-wielding maniac who is threatening to hurt his pregnant wife, while the wife, understandably, retreats and does not help the husband during the fight: the actions of both husband (protecting his wife) and wife (protecting herself) are rightly defined as gynocentric acts. However, if we consider the *overall* relationship between the same husband and wife, we might ask a different question – *is the entire relationship a gyno-centric one?*

If a husband and wife take turns indulging each other across the duration of their relationship in a spirit of ongoing, commensurate reciprocity, then the relationship can be referred to as "couple centered." Conversely, a gyno-*centric* relationship centres predominately or exclusively around the female partner and her wishes. This leads to the conclusion that when there is genuine reciprocity operating within a relationship, a balanced couple-centric dynamic in which the needs, wants and desires of both partners are afforded equal value, it can not be considered a gynocentric relationship (Wright, 2018d).

Much like the power dynamic between a narcissistic and non-narcissistic partner, gynocentric relationships are based on unbalanced roles that are in some ways comparable to master-slave, or BDSM-style relationships (Duits, 2015).

What has been men's role in promoting gynocentric narcissism?

Firstly we can say that men have played a principle role in aiding and abetting the growth of gynocentrism among women, motivated in large part by a desire to form relationships with them. Secondly, as Paul Elam recently pointed out in an article *Daddy's Little Nightmare*, men encourage narcissism in their daughters:

> *It's quite ironic, listening to a man complain about how his wife has crazy unreal expectations. He bemoans the fact that she cannot be satisfied, no matter what he does. He claims that he pulls his hair out trying to figure out how to satisfy her endless demands only to be met with more disapproval and, of course, more demands. He wonders aloud how she ever learned to be such a bottomless pit, and such a bitch about it.*
>
> *Then you go watch him interact with his four-year old daughter, whom he will endlessly coddle and for whom he will go to any measure to make sure she never lacks anything, no matter how trivial.*
>
> *And it doesn't stop when she turns five. Or fifteen, or twenty-five. When it comes to turning human females into paragons of pissy entitlement, the western father has few rivals.* (Elam, 2019)

Suffice to say that many men are complicit in maintaining the status quo, creating a culture of exaggerated benevolent sexism in order to gain romantic access to women. The subsequent relationship dynamic is one they may come to find destructive to their emotional and physical wellbeing and thus unsustainable in the long term. Some men adjust to the gynocentric dynamic by resigning their dreams and emotional needs and playing the role of what is disparagingly referred to as a 'simp' or overly servile partner, perhaps rationalizing that gynocentrism is encoded into our genome and is thus 'the way of nature.'

Gynocentrism is further upheld by men at the institutional level, relying for example on a chivalric compact between women and male politicians who wish to hold office (Farrell, 1996; Frasure-Yokley, 2018;Lodders & Weldon, 2019; Naurin, et al., 2019; Wright, 2017), or male court judges who are eager to demonstrate their chivalric credentials by providing lighter sentences for female offenders (Visher, 1983; Hood, 1992; Curry, et al., 2004; Embry, et al., 2012; Starr, 2015). Such displays by men in positions of power have the effect of normalizing gynocentrism, with the gender imbalance it entails, as an acceptable standard of behavior for heterosexual exchanges.

In cultures perceived as encouraging gynocentrism, an emerging male demographic is seeking female partners who eschew the gynocentric blueprint in favor of alternative relationship models; for example traditional gender roles based on division of responsibility and labor (Wright, 2020), or alternatively a 'multi-option' model for both male and female partners based on the libertarian principles of individual choice, self-determination, and negotiated labor-sharing arrangements (Wright, 2020).

Further, increasing numbers of 'no gynocentrism' men are choosing to avoid long-term relationships with women, adopting instead the lifestyle of confirmed bachelors while engaging in meaningful relationships and activities that can fill the breach (Smith, 2013, Yiannopoulos, 2014). In Western societies these men are sometimes referred to as 'Zeta Males' who reject the gynocentrism-dependent male categories of *alpha* and *beta* (Tayo, 2017), or alternatively they are called 'Men Going Their Own Way,' (Wright & Elam, 2013), and in Japanese society they are given the title of *sôshoku danshi* or 'herbivore men' to denote their refusal to seek traditional 'carnivorous' pursuits of career and women (Smith, 2013, Morioka, 2013, Yiannopoulos, 2014).

Discussion and conclusion

Most academic studies find that males as a group score higher on narcissism scales than do females (Grijalva, et al., 2015). However, these findings may be misleading because the instruments used, their factor structures, and the wording of questionnaires may be more effective at tapping male expressions of narcissism over female expressions within the alternative context of intimate relationships.

Men's typical commitment to work and to learning new skills provides a sense of mastery and competence that is often backed by 'commensurate achievements,' thus men's display of agentic confidence in the area of skill-acquisition may serve as a misleading marker for narcissistic inflation. Conversely, the male social role may encourage a façade of ego-strength in order for men to gain acceptance as reliable laborers, leaders, parents or husbands (Carroll, 1989; Wood & Eagly, 2012; Grijalva, et.al., 2015). In this respect male displays of confidence are aimed substantively toward service roles, and to the generating of resources that can be shared with others. On the downside, a persona of strength may belie an inner feeling of impotence that is considered taboo for public exposure – as men are expected to appear agentic and confident. The fragility of this position is summarized in Dr. Warren Farrell's statement that *'Men's greatest weakness is their façade of strength, and women's greatest strength is their façade of weakness.'* (Farrell, 1996, p. 27).

A finding of gender bias in descriptions and assessment criteria for narcissism have been raised in studies by Akhtar (1982), Philipson (1985), and again in a paper by Carroll (1989) which concluded that the Narcissistic Personality Inventory (NPI) pays more attention to behaviors typifying male expressions of narcissism than female. Carroll states, *"women may exhibit both adaptive and maladaptive narcissism in subtler, more oblique ways than men... [and] may be more likely to express narcissism in an interpersonal style which involves greater enmeshment and dependency upon relationships."* (Carroll, 1989, p.1005). Following Carroll, the main instrument under examination for generating gender bias is the Narcissistic Personality

Inventory (NPI; Raskin & Terry, 1988) which remains the most popular measure of narcissism, employed in over three-quarters of empirical studies (Cain et al., 2008).

The problem of bias in the NPI was recently confirmed by Gebauer et.al (2012), and Nehrlich et.al (2019) who suggest the need to employ a 'two spheres' approach characterized by 'agentic narcissism' and 'communal narcissism,' which tend to be correlated with typical expressions of masculine and feminine gender roles respectively. According to Gebauer et.al, *"acknowledging the existence of a communal facet of narcissism broadens the scope of narcissistic self-affirmation, self-promotion, and self-enhancement. In other words, the agency-communion model supports the existence of... situation-behavior patterns among narcissists that extend into the communal domain."* (2012, p.871)

These studies lend support to the contention that women's expression of narcissism can be more relational in nature, requiring alternative constructs and scales to assess. Furthermore, women's narcissism may be highly targeted in its communal expression because women might not feel entitled, for example, to special treatment by all non-intimate males nor by other women, whereas they may feel highly entitled to special treatment by men and boys in platonic and intimate relationships, as detailed above. To effectively measure female narcissism, otherwise referred to in this essay as *gynocentrism*, new scales need to be developed to target the specific behaviors outlined and the contexts in which they typically occur.

This essay demonstrates that the DSM-5 criteria for Narcissistic Personality Disorder is significantly correlated with behaviors and expectations of gynocentric women, which leads to the conclusion that gynocentrism is a gendered expression of narcissism operating in the limiting context of heterosexual relations.

References

Akhtar, S., & Thomson, J. A. (1982). Overview: Narcissistic personality disorder. *The American journal of psychiatry*.

American Psychiatric Association. (2013). *Diagnostic and statistical manual of mental disorders (DSM-5®)*. American Psychiatric Pub.

Banja, J. D. (2005). *Medical errors and medical narcissism*. Jones & Bartlett Learning.

Belenky, M. F., Clinchy, B. M., Goldberger, N. R., & Tarule, J. M. (1986). *Women's ways of knowing: The development of self, voice, and mind* (Vol. 15). New York: Basic books.

Birmingham, G. A. (1914) *From Dublin to Chicago: Some Notes on a Tour in America*. George H. Doran Company

Cain, N. M., Pincus, A. L., & Ansell, E. B. (2008). Narcissism at the crossroads: Phenotypic description of pathological narcissism across clinical theory, social/personality psychology, and psychiatric diagnosis. *Clinical psychology review, 28*(4), 638-656.

Campbell, W. K., & Miller, J. D. (2011). *The handbook of narcissism and narcissistic personality disorder: Theoretical approaches, empirical findings, and treatments*. John Wiley & Sons.

Carroll, L. (1989). A comparative study of narcissism, gender, and sex-role orientation among bodybuilders, athletes, and psychology students. *Psychological Reports, 64*(3), 999-1006.

Collins, W. (2016) *The Empathy Gap*, article published at The Illustrated Empathy Gap. http://empathygap.uk

Curry, T. R., Lee, G., & Rodriguez, S. F. (2004). Does victim gender increase sentence severity? Further explorations of gender dynamics and sentencing outcomes. *Crime & Delinquency, 50*(3), 319-343.

Davis, C. (2010). *Charlotte Perkins Gilman: A Biography*. Stanford University Press.

De Zavala, A. G., Cichocka, A., Eidelson, R., & Jayawickreme, N. (2009). Collective narcissism and its social consequences. *Journal of personality and social psychology*, *97*(6), 1074.

Dictionary, M. W. (2020) Merriam-Webster Dictionary. (Retrieved March 23, 2020, from https://www.merriam-webster.com/dictionary/gynocentric)

Dictionary, O. E. (2008). *Oxford English Dictionary*. Oxford University Press. (Retrieved March,18, 2020 from https://www.lexico.com/definition/gynocentric)

Dictionary S. D. (2016). K. Bell (Ed.), *Open education sociology dictionary*. (Retrieved March, 18, 2020 from https://sociologydictionary.org/gynocentrism/)

Dictionary, Y (2018). *YourDictionary*. Retrieved March, 18, 2020 from https://www.yourdictionary.com/gynocentrism)

Duits, E. J. (2015). *L'autre désir: du sadomasochisme à l'amour courtois*. la Musardine.

Elam, Paul. (2016). *Gynocentrism: The Root of Feminism*, speech delivered to International Conference on Men's Issues, London.

Elam, P., & Tieman, A. (March 2018) *Discussing Gynocentrism | HBR Debate 7 | Youtube*

Elam, Paul. (2019). *Daddy's Little Nightmare*, published at A Voice for Men. (https://avoiceformen.com/)

Embry, R., & Lyons Jr, P. M. (2012). Sex-based sentencing: Sentencing discrepancies between male and female sex offenders. *Feminist Criminology*, *7*(2), 146-162.

Encyclopedia R. (2005) "Gynocentrism." In *Encyclopedia of Religion*. (Retrieved March 23, 2020 from Encyclopedia.com: https://www.encyclopedia.com/environment/encyclopedias-almanacs-transcripts-and-maps/gynocentrism)

Farrell, W. (1996). *The myth of male power*. Berkeley Publishing Group.

Fenichel, O. (1938). The drive to amass wealth. *The Psychoanalytic Quarterly*, 7(1), 69-95.

Fiamengo, J. (2015) *The Empathy Gap* – Fiamengo File Episode 4, YouTube. https://youtu.be/MKJ8x9ut1hU

Frasure-Yokley, L. (2018). Choosing the Velvet Glove: Women Voters, Ambivalent Sexism, and Vote Choice in 2016. *Journal of Race, Ethnicity and Politics*, 3(1), 3-25.

Freud, S. (1914). *On Narcissism*. The Standard Edition of the Complete Psychological Works of Sigmund Freud. *Trans. and ed. James Strachey*, 14, pp. 67-102.

Freud, S. (1991). *Sigmund Freud: Introductory Lectures on Psychoanalysis*. pp. 471-72. Penguin.

Friday, N. (1996). *The power of beauty*. London: Hutchinson

Galbi, D. (2015). Cultural construction of Reddy's The Making of Romantic Love (2015), and. *Musa iocosa: vital medieval poetic medicine for pedestalizing women*. Published by *Purple Motes*. https://www.purplemotes.net/

Gebauer, J. E., Sedikides, C., Verplanken, B., & Maio, G. R. (2012). Communal narcissism. *Journal of Personality and Social Psychology*, 103(5), 854.

Gilligan, C. (1993). *In a different voice: Psychological theory and women's development*. Harvard University Press.

Gilman, C. P. (1898). *In this our world*. Small, Maynard.

Gilman, C. P. (1911a). The Man-Made World; or. *Our Androcentric Culture*.

Gilman, C. P. (1911b). *Moving the Mountain*. Charlton Company.

Gouws, D. S. (2018). Not So Romantic for Men: Using Sir Walter Scott's Ivanhoe to Explore Evolving Notions of Chivalry and Their Impact on Twenty-First-Century Manhood. In *Voicing the Silences of Social and Cognitive Justice* (pp. 167-178). Brill Sense.

Grijalva, E., Newman, D. A., Tay, L., Donnellan, M. B., Harms, P. D., Robins, R. W., & Yan, T. (2015). Gender differences in narcissism: A meta-analytic review. *Psychological bulletin, 141*(2), 261.

Hammond, M. D., Sibley, C. G., & Overall, N. C. (2014). *The allure of sexism: Psychological entitlement fosters women's endorsement of benevolent sexism over time.* Social Psychological and Personality Science, 5(4), pp. 422 - 429.

Hood, R. G. (1992). *Race and sentencing: a study in the Crown Court: a report for the Commission for Racial Equality*. Oxford University Press, USA.

Jarosek, S. (2017). *Transcending Scientism: Mending Broken Culture's Broken Science*. Lulu Press, Inc.

Kohut, H., & Tolpin, P. (1996). *The Chicago institute lectures*. Hillsdale, NJ: Analytic Press.

Kostakis, A. (2011a). Lecture 2: *The Same Old Gynocentric Story*, Gynocentrism theory Lectures, (retrieved from gynocentrism.com on 22/03/20)

Kostakis, A. (2011b). Lecture 11. *The Eventual Outcome of Feminism, Part II*, Gynocentrism theory Lectures, (retrieved from gynocentrism.com on 22/03/20)

Kostakis, A. (2011c). Lecture 4. *Pig Latin*, Gynocentrism theory Lectures (retrieved from gynocentrism.com on 22/03/20)

Lambe, S., Hamilton-Giachritsis, C., Garner, E., & Walker, J. (2018). The role of narcissism in aggression and violence: A systematic review. *Trauma, Violence, & Abuse, 19*(2), 209-230.

Lasch, C. (2018). *The culture of narcissism: American life in an age of diminishing expectations*. WW Norton & Company.

Levin, J. D. (1995). *Slings and arrows: Narcissistic injury and its treatment*. Jason Aronson, Incorporated.

Lodders, V., & Weldon, S. (2019). Why do women vote radical right? Benevolent sexism, representation and inclusion in four countries. *Representation, 55*(4), 457-474.

McSweeny, L. (2018). *It's Official: Power Creates A Narcissist*. Pursuit, Inside Business, University of Melbourne

Morioka, M. (2013). A phenomenological study of "herbivore men".

Nathanson, P., & Young, K. K. (2001). *Spreading misandry: The teaching of contempt for men in popular culture*. McGill-Queen's Press-MQUP.

Nathanson, P. & Young, K. K. (2006). *Legalizing Misandry* (pp. 309-316) McGill-Queen's University Press.

Nathanson, P. & Young, K. K. (2010). *Sanctifying Misandry*, McGill-Queen's University Press.

Naurin, D., Naurin, E., and Amy A. (2019). *Gender Stereotyping and Chivalry in International Negotiations: A Survey Experiment in the Council of the European Union*. A Survey Experiment in the Council of the European Union. International Organization, 73(2), pp. 469-488.
Ovid. (1916). *Metamorphoses, with an English Translation by Frank Justus Miller*. W. Heinemann.

Nehrlich, A. D., Gebauer, J. E., Sedikides, C., & Schoel, C. (2019). Agentic narcissism, communal narcissism, and prosociality. *Journal of Personality and Social Psychology, 117*(1), 142.

Philipson, I. (1985). Gender and narcissism. *Psychology of women quarterly*, 9(2), 213-228.

Plante, T. G. (Ed.). (2006). *Mental disorders of the new millennium* (Vol. 1). pp. 43-44.Greenwood Publishing Group.

Raskin, R., & Terry, H. (1988). A principal-components analysis of the Narcissistic Personality Inventory and further evidence of its construct validity. *Journal of personality and social psychology*, 54(5), 890.

Reber, A. S. (1995). 'Narcissistic injury,' definition in*The Penguin dictionary of psychology*. Penguin Press

Reich, A. (1953). Narcissistic object choice in women. *Journal of the American Psychoanalytic Association*, 1(1), 22-44.

Ronningstam, E. (2005). *Identifying and understanding the narcissistic personality*. Oxford University Press.

Ryan, P. (2018) *Diagnosing Gynocentrism*. Essay. (retrieved from gynocentrism.com on 22/03/20)

Schoenewolf, G. (2017) *Feminism and 'gender narcissism,'* published on *A Voice for Men* website.

Schwartz-Salant, N. (1982). *Narcissism and character transformation: The psychology of narcissistic character disorders* (Vol. 9). Inner City Books.

Sherrill, S.(Dec 9, 2001). Acquired Situational Narcissism, interview with Robert B. Millman. *New York Times*.

Smith, H. (2013). *Men on Strike: Why Men are Boycotting Marriage, Fatherhood, and the American Dream--and why it Matters*. Encounter Books.

Starr, S. B. (2015). Estimating gender disparities in federal criminal cases. *American Law and Economics Review, 17*(1), 127-159.

Tayo, A. O. (2017) *A new class of men who don't care what you think - Zeta Males are the new type of men who do not play the 'game' but are societal rebels.* Published at Pulse.ng.

Twenge, J. (2009). Generation Me (2006) and. *The Narcissism Epidemic.*

Tyler, I. (2005). 'Who put the "Me" in feminism?' The sexual politics of narcissism. *Feminist Theory, 6*(1), 25-44.

Visher, C. A. (1983). Gender, police arrest decisions, and notions of chivalry. *Criminology, 21*(1), 5-28.

Ward, L. F. (1888). *Our better halves.*

Ward, L. F. (1903). *Pure sociology: A treatise on the origin and spontaneous development of society.* Macmillan Company.

Wallace, W. C. Gibson, C. Gordon, N. A. Lakhan, R. Mahabir, J. and Seetahal. C. (2019). *Domestic Violence: Intimate Partner Violence Victimization Non-Reporting to the Police in Trinidad and Tobago.* Justice Policy Journal.

Wood, W., & Eagly, A. H. (2012). Biosocial construction of sex differences and similarities in behavior. In *Advances in experimental social psychology* (Vol. 46, pp. 55-123). Academic Press.

Wright, P. Elam, P. (2013), *Go Your Own Way: Understanding MGTOW.* Zeta Press.

Wright, P. (2014). *Gynocentrism: From Feudalism to the Modern Disney Princess.* Academic Century Press.

Wright, P. (2016). *Damseling, Chivalry and Courtly Love.* Published at https://gynocentrism.com/ (retrieved on 22/03/20)

Wright, P. (Ed.). (2017). Republicans and Democrats, both Gynocrats. Chapter 8. *A Brief History of The Men's Rights Movement: From 1856 to the present.* Academic Century Press.

Wright, P. (2018a). Governance Feminism: A Review, Chapter 2, *Feminism and The Creation of a Female Aristocracy.* Academic Century Press.

Wright, P. (2018b). *Bastardized Chivalry: From Concern For Weakness To Sexual Exploitation*, New Male Studies: An International Journal ISSN 1839-7816 ~ Vol 7 Issue 2,2018, pp. 43–59. Australian Institute of Male Health and Studies.

Wright, P. (2018c). *Feminism and The Creation of a Female Aristocracy.* Academic Century Press.

Wright, P. (2018d). *What's in a suffix? taking a closer look at the word gyno–centrism.* Published at https://gynocentrism.com/ (retrieved on 22/03/20)

Wright, P. (2019). Aggrieved Entitlement – women's reaction to temporary loss of chivalry. Chapter 8. *Chivalry: A Gynocentric Tradition.* Academic Century Press.

Wright, P. (2020). *Tradwives, Modwives and Feminists*, Published at https://gynocentrism.com/ (retrieved on 22/03/20)

Yiannopoulos, M. (2014). The sexodus, part 1: The men giving up on women and checking out of society. *Breitbart London.*

Young, I. M. (1985, January). Humanism, gynocentrism and feminist politics. In *Women's Studies International Forum* (Vol. 8, No. 3, pp. 173-183). Pergamon.

12. A Sentimental Continuation of Coverture

Most of us have observed the baffling refusal of women to take responsibility for mistakes, or for outright shitty behavior. More accurately said, we've all observed women's tendency to impute responsibility for their transgressions to others; especially to men. Thousands of people recognize the tendency; they discuss it, make jokes about it, suffer it in their marriages, and every single day you can read hundreds of new anecdotes demonstrating it in action. In short, *it's definitely a thing.*

Where the hell does does this behavior originate?

Some might view it as a genetic tendency, that women's refusal to take responsibility arises from a genetic peculiarity. Or perhaps we might garner a pretzel-shaped argument from an Evolutionary Psychologist suggesting that women's shirking of responsibility is a necessary sexual or survival strategy. Unfortunately such hypotheses do little more than mirror the usual traditionalist attempts at absolving women of responsibility.

For this article I'm going to pose a simpler, culturally rooted explanation: *coverture.*

The doctrine of coverture, in its most basic definition, dictates that husbands are to take responsibility for wives' wellbeing, and also to suffer proxy punishment for her social and legal transgressions – all responsibility rests with the husband whether he likes it or not.

As a social policy, the doctrine of coverture began to develop from approximately the 11th century, gaining currency throughout the British Isles from where it was imported to the wider world via English colonies. Douglas Galbi summarises the intent of coverture as follows:

Coverture was the idea that husband and wife are one under law. More specifically, coverture assigned to the husband responsibility and punishment under law for his wife's criminal acts. Coverture also protected women from mass imprisonment for debt in early modern England...

Coverture was among a range of institutions and ideas that generated highly disproportionate imprisonment of men. Legal history conventionally interprets coverture as a legal concept oppressing women. Coverture oppressed women in the same way that men-only Selective Service registration oppresses women today...

Coverture has been badly misunderstood in legal history. Coverture assigned to husbands responsibility for their wives' criminal acts and their wives' debts. Coverture increased the criminalization of men... Anti-men bias in invoking coverture is a general rhetorical pattern built upon deep structures of gynocentrism.[1]

According to the Oxford Dictionary, *coverture* originally referred to anything used as a cover, such as a shelter, the lid of a cup or dish, the cover of a book, or the cover of a bed, and is synonymous with the general and collective sense of *'covering.'*

In its wider sense, the purpose of a coverture is described as any device used to provide protection, shelter, or adornment. Interestingly, it can also mean *to conceal* as in a veil or disguise used to foster covert conduct or to deceive. In the latter sense coverture "covers a multitude of sins," thereby offering a pretense, a justification, and a defense for egregious conduct.

The social doctrine of coverture saw that men "covered" for women's sins in exchange for the husband's supposed privilege of authority; a privilege we could justifiably read as a poisoned chalice when one considers the number of men that went to the gallows in place of their wives.

Fast forward to the 19th century when coverture laws were still in place, and the advent of feminism was beginning. Feminists hit upon a plan to remove the "male authority" facet of the coverture doctrine, but to retain the "male responsibility for women's wrongdoing" aspect of it. In effect they split coverture down the middle, trashing one half of the doctrine and continuing to preserve the other. As E. B. Bax observed:

> *"For it is a significant and amusing fact that no mention is ever made by the advocate of women's claims of the privileges which have always been accorded the "weaker sex." These privileges are quietly pocketed as a matter of course, without any sort of acknowledgment, much less any suggestion of surrender."*
> Some Heterodox Notes on the Women Question (1887)

> *"This public opinion regards it as axiomatic that women are capable of everything men are capable of, that they ought to have full responsibility in all honourable and lucrative functions and callings. There is only one thing for which unlimited allowance ought to be made on the ground of their otherwise non-existent womanly inferiority, and that is their own criminal or tortious acts! In a word, they are not to be held responsible, in the sense that men are, for their own actions when these entail unpleasant consequences for themselves. On the contrary, the obloquy and, where possible, the penalty for the wrong-doing is to be shifted on to the nearest wretched man with whom they have consorted."*
> Why I Am an Anti-Suffragist (1909)

> *"To men all duties and no rights, to women all rights and no duties, is the basic principle underlying Modern Feminism, Suffragism, and the bastard chivalry it is so fond of invoking."*
> The Fraud of Feminism, Chapter VII: The Psychology of the Movement (1913)

Further to Bax's claim that the penalty for women's wrongdoing got shifted onto the nearest wretched man, we appear to have come in the 21st century to not only maintaining, but amplifying the blame game in an effort to retain the "dignity, esteem, and reputation" of today's women — a blame game that has its unbroken root in the tradition of coverture.

If the theory of ongoing-coverture satisfies the baffling question of why women shirk responsibility, then we at least have an answer. Women want to maintain the historical tradition of having their transgressions excised, hidden and covered by men, while they go about securing the gynocentric utopia they have been so effective at building.

Maintenance of sentimental coverture rightly belongs to gynocentrism theory. For how could gynocentrism survive if women took more responsibility, if they were more accountable for their acts? Quite simply gynocentrism couldn't survive on that basis, particularly if their aim is one of fairness and equality which can only be achieved by truly emancipating women and holding them responsible for their actions.

So as a working model lets add *sentimental coverture* as one of 5 pillars of a gynocentric temple, which would look something like this: Pillar-1. Chivalry, 2. Courtly/romantic love, 3. Gender narcissism, 4. Coverture, and lastly 5. Power-seeking (via the long march through the institutions of power, this strategy being evident for centuries before Marxism was dreamed up, as for example in the writing of Christine De Pizan and her *'City of Ladies'*).

In summary, this article posits that coverture has survived long beyond its historical use in law, becoming a social custom divested of its original legal framework. Whatever the merits of its original purpose, the sentimental continuation of coverture provides an enduring custom encouraging women's shirking of personal responsibility – this thanks in no small part to the activism of the feminist movement which postures as progressive, but turns out to be the same as it ever was.

References:

[1] Galbi, Douglass, *Coverture, Domestic Violence & Criminalization of Men* (2015)

PART THREE

Rituals of Romance

13. The Art of Attraction

In 1991 Naomi Wolf wrote *The Beauty Myth* where she claimed that women are oppressed by cultural pressure to be beautiful. What she failed to tell us is where this habit originated, and more importantly, how it is essentially used to increase female power and influence over others – men especially.

In human beings, various compulsions and desires come into conflict with one another, each jostling for momentary supremacy where one imperative will usurp the claims of another. That game has reached a problematical impasse during the last 800 years because, during that relatively short time span, human culture has thrown the weight of its patronage into developing, intensifying and enforcing sexual gamesmanship to the degree that our sexual compulsions appear pumped up on steroids and taken to extremes never before seen in human society (myths about widespread Roman orgies notwithstanding). The obsession with female beauty forms a significant part of the problem.

If we lived back in Ancient Greece, Rome or anywhere else we would view sexual intercourse as little more than a bodily function akin to eating, shitting and sleeping – a basic bodily function without the hype. After the Middle Ages, however, it developed into a commodity to pimp and trade, and the new cult of sexualized romance that arose from it resulted in a frustration of our more basic attachment needs – a frustration aided and abetted by social institutions placing sexual manipulation at the center of human interactions. This development entrenched a new belief that beauty was the native possession of women, and only women, and conversely that the desire to possess beauty was the lot of males alone, thus creating a division between the sexes that remains in place today.

Compare this division with the beliefs of older cultures – India, Rome, Greece etc – and we see a stark contrast, with classical cultures equally apportioning beauty to males and sexual desire to females. In ancient Greece for example males used to grow their hair long and comb it adoringly, rub olive oil on their skin and pay devoted attention to attire -the colors of the toga, the materials it was woven from, the way it was draped on the body- and there is perhaps no modern culture on earth where male beauty is more marvelously celebrated in the arts than it was in Greece.

Another example comes from the Biblical Song of Solomon, in which the appreciation of beauty and associated longing flows both ways between the man and women, whereas in romantic love beauty is ascribed only to the female, and desire only to the male – the roles are radically split. Moreover, in the Song of Songs there is no hint of the gynocentric arrangement; no appearance of man as a vassal towards women who are both Lord and deity. For the lovers in Song of Songs there already exists a God and so there is no worshipping of the woman as a quasi divinity who can redeem the man's pathetic existence – as in "romantic" love.

According to Robert Solomon, romantic love required a dramatic change in the self-conception of women. He recounts;

> They too were freed from an identity that depended wholly on their social roles, that is, their blood and legal ties with men, as daughters, wives and mothers. It is in this period in Christian history that looks become of primary importance, that being beautiful now counts for possibly everything, not just an attractive feature in a daughter or wife (which probably counted very little anyway) but as itself a mark of character, style, personality. Good grooming, as opposed to propriety, came to define the individual woman, and her worth, no longer dependent on the social roles and positions of her father, husband or children, now turned on her looks. The premium was placed on youth and beauty, and though some women even then may have condemned this emphasis as unjust, it at least formed the first breach with a society that, hitherto, had left little room for personal initiative or individual advancement. The prototype of the Playboy playmate, we might say, was already established eight hundred years ago, and did not require, as some people have argued recently, Hugh Hefner's slick centerfolds to make youth, beauty and a certain practiced

vacuity into a highly esteemed personal virtue. The problem is why we still find it difficult to move *beyond* this without, like some Platonists, distaining beauty altogether – the opposite error.[1]

Modesta Pozzo penned a book in the 1500's entitled *The Worth of Women: their Nobility and Superiority to Men*. The work purportedly records a conversation among seven Venetian noblewomen that explores nearly every aspect of women's experience. One of the topics explored is women's use of cosmetics and clothing to enhance beauty, including mention of hair tinting for which there is twenty-six different recipes. The following is the voice of Cornelia who explains that men's sexual desire of women (and women's control of that process via beauty) is the only reason men can love:

> "Thinking about it straight, what more worthy and what lovelier subject can one find than the beauty, grace and virtues of women?… I'd say that a perfectly composed outer corporeal form is something most worthy of our esteem, for it is this visible outer form that is the first to present itself to our eye and our understanding: we see it and instantly love and desire it, prompted by an instinct embedded in us by nature. "It's not because men love us that they go in for all these displays of love and undying devotion, rather, it's because they desire us. So that in this case love is the offspring, desire the parent, or, in other words, love is the effect and desire the cause. And since taking away the cause means taking away the effect, that means that men love us for just as long as they desire us and once desire, which is the cause of their vain love, has died in them (either because they have got what they wanted or because they have realized that they are not going to be able to get it), the love that is the effect of that cause dies at exactly the same time."[2] [written 1592]

What I find interesting is that since the Middle Ages, as evidenced in Cornelia's words, we have collectively conflated male love with sexual desire as if they are inseparable, and to women's ability to control that male "love" through a skillful cultivation of beauty. One might be forgiven for refusing to believe this is love at all, that it is instead the creation of an intense desire for sexual pleasure due to the call of beauty. Observation shows that sex-generated "love" does not necessarily lead to compatibility for partners across a broad range of interests, and may occur between people who are, aside from sexual attraction, totally incompatible, with little in common, which is why the relationship often goes so badly when there occur gaps in the sexual game.

This raises the alternative notion of love based on compatibility, on what we might term 'friendship-love' which is not based solely on sexual desire – in fact sexual desire is not even essential to it though often present. Friendship love is about interests the partners share in common, a meeting of compatible souls and a getting to know each other on a level playing field. However aiming for friendship-love means women are no longer required to pull the strings of sexual desire as is practiced with beauty-based allure, which ultimately frees men and women to meet as equals in power and, with luck, find much in common to sustain a durable relationship.

Sources:

[1] Robert Solomon, Love: Emotion, Myth, Metaphor, 1990 (p.62)
[2] Modesta Pozzo, The Worth of Women: their Nobility and Superiority to Men, 2007

14. Valentine's Day

In the context of gynocentric culture it may be helpful to recount the historical roots of Valentine's Day and highlight the farce that it appears to have become… or perhaps more accurately, *that it has always been.*

Let's begin with a primer about what Valentine's Day means for men, or rather what it *should* mean for men, according to advice columnist and relationship expert Brooke Miller.[1]

Here she addresses men directly:

> **First lesson:** Valentine's Day matters. This really isn't debatable my darlings, just trust me on this one. **Second lesson:** Valentine's Day matters because… Because it's not really about Valentine's Day…it's a metaphor. Really? Yes, really.
>
> Valentine's Day is a metaphor for *every other moment throughout the entire duration of your relationship* when the woman in your life needs and wants and hopes you are able to joyfully and proudly step out of your way, and *make it about her.*
>
> Valentine's Day is a holiday decorated with girly-pink-sparkly-chocolate-flowery-hearts…and and and. February 14th could not be less stereotypically masculine if it tried. Although this holiday may not be about you, it is in fact, *for you*. It gifts you the opportunity to demonstrate the kind of guy you can be when put in a situation that is *not about you*. It shows that beautiful human being you're lucky to be with that you, you amazing man, are able to *show up selflessly to any occasion.*
>
> Valentine's Day gives your crush or girlfriend or fiancé or wife, either a taste or a reminder (women love being reminded) of your ability to care about things not because *you* care about

them, but because you *care about her*… and she cares about things. Get it?

Women know very well that Valentine's Day doesn't particularly matter to you, but *making* it matter to you, simply and solely *for her*… now that's a guy worth being with.

An acknowledgment of the day, a card, flowers, or even a romantic gift like a massage or spa treatment (hint hint) shows your capacity to put yourself aside even if she doesn't ask you to–especially if she doesn't ask you to… and put her first.[1]

* * *

So there you have it gents; on Valentine's Day step the fuck out of your own way and make it all about her, and while you are at it get rid of your preconceived notions that say love is meant to be *bi-directional*. And if you end up marrying one of the many narcissistic princesses who expect this kind of treatment make sure to remember that the day of your marriage, too, is "her day." In fact why beat around the bush – marriage to her will mean every single day of the rest of your life will probably be "her days" too.

But getting back to Valentine's Day, lets take a little look at the background of this gynocentric event.

Valentine's Day, the celebration of romantic love, first became popular in the High Middle Ages when the traditions of courtly love arose, and has been celebrated as a holiday ever since. However the precise origins of the concept are somewhat unclear, and the situation is made more complicated by the fact that there are no less than three Saint Valentines in the historical folklore.

The first written Valentine note was believed to be by Charles the Duke of Orleans who in 1415 AD, while imprisoned in the Tower of London, sent a love letter to his wife. An excerpt from that letter still exists in the British Library's collection and reads "I am already sick from love, My very gentle Valentine." The date became further associated with romantic and courtly love when Geoffrey Chaucer incorporated St. Valentine's Day into his love poem "The Parliament of Foules." Chaucer, who wrote the love poem to commemorate the engagement of Richard II and Anne of Bohemia, linked the royal engagement with the pairing of birds and Valentine's Day. The holiday was also mentioned in Shakespeare's Hamlet, as well as by the poet John Donne, and has since evolved into what most would now consider the most romantic day of the year. Perhaps the most famous Valentine's poem is this one published in *Gammer Gurton's Garland*, a 1784 collection of English rhymes:

The rose is red, the violet's blue,
The honey's sweet, and so are you.
Thou are my love and I am thine;
I drew thee to my Valentine:
The lot was cast and then I drew,
And Fortune said it shou'd be you.

The tradition of exchanging gifts and tokens was established during the height of romantic love when people began to select their own Valentine's mates, and the tradition began to appear frequently in love poetry. The elaborate exchanges of poetry, cards, and gifts cemented it as a holiday for the celebration of love in European popular culture. Valentine's Day has since spread all over the world, and most nations still celebrate it on the 14th of February with flowers, gifts, and cards.

The soil in which the celebration bloomed celebrated love as illicit, passionate, morally elevating, transcendent, if at times painful and humiliating: the perfect recipe for an affair. Participants adopted the language of feudalism with chivalric men declaring themselves "love servants" who pledged themselves in submission, obedience, and utility to ladies whom they worshipped as both their overlord and moral superior. This feudalisation of love -so called by C.S. Lewis- was popularized by troubadours in poems and songs, providing both the model and the spirit we continue to express on Valentine's Day.

"Valentine's Day gives your crush or girlfriend or fiancé or wife, either a taste or a reminder of your ability to care about **things** not because you care about them, but because you care about her… and she cares about **things**."[1]

By the 18th century it had become a widespread custom for men in all social classes to exchange small tokens of affection or handwritten notes on February 14. In the Victorian era, printed cards replaced written letters as a way to express emotions, encouraged both by improvements in printing technology and cheaper postage rates. In the 1840s, Esther A. Howland began to sell the first mass-produced valentines in America. This practice was extended in the 20th century to all manners of gifts, especially in the United States. With the advent of consumerism in post-war America, Valentine's Day became a day of gift-giving, from roses and chocolates to diamonds, and the immense popularity of the event tells us that the spirit of chivalry and courtly love is far indeed from being over.

While some couples might equally indulge each other on this auspicious occasion, more often than not it will be a day on which the man will worship a woman as his true overlord, with himself playing the role of gift-giving serf. Perhaps Valentine's Day will one day be worth celebrating if it becomes a reciprocal event, but until then the best advice for men on ~~Vagina Day~~ Valentine's Day will be to reframe the event as *Go Your Own Way Day.*

Source:

[1] Brooke on Boys: Why Valentine's Day Matters, in *Primer Magazine: A Guy's Post-College Guide to Growing Up.* (Retrieved 09/02/2014 http://www.primermagazine.com/2010/love/brooke-on-boys-why-valentines-day-matters)

15. Rituals of Marriage

Modern marriage evolved from a historical ritual designed to indenture slaves to masters, though most people have forgotten its history. However, many of the behaviours and rituals central to this history can still be discerned in modern marriage.

The Ring

It's thought that the practice of exchanging wedding rings extends far back into ancient history, with evidence of the ritual being found in Ancient Egypt, Rome, and within several religious cultures. However *our* modern-day practice of giving wedding rings has a very different origin and meaning, one which may make you, well, cringe a little. As suggested on the Society of Phineas blog, the ring functions as a feudalistic contract between the man and his wife:

> "The ring functions as a proof of ability in the supplicant vassal's pledge to the wife. This is true given the traditional expectation of the amount of resources to be expended in purchasing the ring along with providing for the wedding day. In this gynocentric environment, it's total sacrilege to not present a woman with her One Ring or to present one that is substandard to her or her friends. She uses her One Ring as a social proof of her status around Team Woman (it's a competition much like Valentine's Day gifts), as she will not hesitate to show it off as much as possible when she first gets it if it meets with her approval." [1]

This contention finds support from medievalist scholars who show the origin of our ring-exchanging ritual in early literary sources and artistic depictions of the Middle Ages. H.J. Chaytor, for instance wrote "The lover was formally installed as such by the lady, took an oath of fidelity to her and received a kiss to seal it, a ring or some other personal possession."[2] Professor Joan Kelly gives us a summary of the practice:

"A kiss (like the kiss of homage) sealed the pledge, rings were exchanged, and the knight entered the love service of his lady. Representing love along the lines of vassalage had several liberating implications for aristocratic women. Most fundamental, ideas of homage and mutuality entered the notion of heterosexual relations along with the idea of freedom. As symbolized on shields and other illustrations that place the knight in the ritual attitude of commendation, kneeling before his lady with his hands folded between hers, homage signified male service, not domination or subordination of the lady, and it signified fidelity, constancy in that service." [3]

Like the description given by Kelly, men continue to go down on one knee and are quick to demonstrate humility by claiming the wedding is "her day", betraying the origin and conception of marriage as more feudalistic in its structure than Christian. With gestures like these it's obvious that modern marriage is based on the earlier feudalistic ritual known as a 'commendation ceremony' whereby a bond between a lord and his fighting man (ie. his vassal) was created. The commendation ceremony is composed of two elements, one to perform the act of homage and the other an oath of fealty. For the Oath of fealty ceremony the vassal would place his hands on a Bible (as is still practiced) and swear he would never injure his overlord in any way and would remain faithful. Once the vassal had sworn the oath of fealty, the lord and vassal had a feudal relationship.

Because this archaic contract remains current in contemporary marriages, we might also question our typical concepts of *obeyance* between a husband and wife. In older Christian ceremonies the women sometimes vowed to love, cherish and "obey" her husband. However, because framed within a feudalistic-style relationship the woman's obeyance was strongly offset and perhaps overturned in practice because she tended to be the dominant power-holder in relation to the man. In the latter case the wife as more powerful figure is merely obeying -if she is obeying anything at all- her responsibilities as a kindly overlord to her husband. Notice here that we have switched from the notion of a benevolent patriarchy to a kindly gynocentrism which feminists like to promote as loving, nurturing, peace-loving and egalitarian.

Love service

The Medieval model of service to a feudal lord was transferred wholesale into relationships as "love service" of men toward ladies. Such service is the hallmark of romantic love and is characterized by men's deference to a woman who is viewed as a moral superior. During this period women were often referred to by men as *domnia* (dominant rank), *midons* (my lord), and later *dame* (honored authority) which terms each draw their root from the Latin *dominus* meaning "master," or "owner," particularly of slaves. Medieval language expert Peter Makin confirms that the men who used these terms must have been aware of what they were saying:

> "William IX calls his lady midons, which I have translated as 'my Lord'... These men knew their Latin and must have been aware of its origins and peculiarity; in fact it was clearly their collective emotions and expectations that drew what amounts to a metaphor from the area of lordship, just as it is the collective metaphor-making process that establishes 'baby' as a term for a girlfriend and that creates and transforms language constantly. In the same way, knowing that *Dominus* was the standard term for God, and that *don*, 'lord', was also used for God, they must also have felt some connection with religious adoration.[4]

Recapitulation

Let's recapitulate the practices associated with the ring-giving ritual of marriage:

1. Genuflection: man goes down on one knee to propose
2. Commendation token: rings exchanged
3. Vassal's kiss: reenacted during the ceremony
4. Homage and fealty: implicit in marriage vows
5. Subservience: "It's her special day"
6. Service: man prepares to work for wife for his whole life
7. Disposability: "I would die for you".

Is it any wonder that women are so eager to get married and that men are rejecting marriage in droves?[5] The feudalistic model reveals exactly what men are buying into via that little golden band – a life commitment to a woman culturally primed to act as our overlord. As more men become aware of this travesty they will choose to reject it, and for those still considering marriage I encourage you to read this article a second time; your ability to keep or lose your freedom depends upon it.

References:

[1] Website: Society of Phineas (Retrieved 29/04/2014 from http://societyofphinas.wordpres.com/2013/04/16/the-one-ring-to-rule-over-him/)
[2] H.J. Chaytor, *The Troubadours* (1913)
[3] Joan Kelly, *Women, History, and Theory*, University of Chicago Press, 1986
[4] Peter Makin, *Provence and Pound*, University of California Press, 1978
[5] Helen Smith, Men on Strike: *Why Men Are Boycotting Marriage, Fatherhood, and the American Dream - and Why It Matters*, Encounter Books, 2013

16. Down The Aisle Again

Once again I find myself walking into the murky waters of marriage, this time not in real life but in print, praise angels. As mentioned in a recent article by August Løvenskiolds, we had a conversation about marriage which unearthed some alternative ways of looking at it. On several points our understanding aligned, and on others they diverged. So rather than rely on August's article alone, I'd like to lay down my own thoughts.

The conversation was partly stimulated by a comment I made elsewhere, which we decided to unpack – and I hope to unpack it further in this article:

Aside from those differences over origins, both sides agree that gynocentric marriage – its culture, customs, laws, taboos – must be utterly abandoned, not reformed. Notice here I refer to *gynocentric* marriage and not to a marriage of the minds, hearts, dreams, goals, projects, and bodies that might come with non-gynocentric relationships.

The contention of this paragraph is, hypothetically speaking, that a marriage can be based on different priorities than those of gynocentrism. But before getting into it further lets start with the widest definition of marriage from the Oxford Dictionary, which is:

"any intimate association or union"

This definition covers pretty much all unions in which two or more things are brought together – whether in physics, biology, linguistics, or culture. In this case we are referring to human unions, and while some of the accompanying customs and behavior go well beyond this basic definition, they each conform to this minimum requirement in order to satisfy for the label marriage.

There are two main orders of human union to consider: one involving culturally prescribed marriage customs, vs. the unadorned biological demand for intimate association.

During our discussion, and in his recent article, August proposed several combinations of words (portmanteaus) to describe different kinds of marriage. For the sake of simplicity I'm only going to tackle the two primary terms which are *Gynomarriage*, and *Biomarriage*.

Gynomarriage

Gynomarriage, (portmanteau of gynocentrism + marriage) describes the typical union between a men and women today. It is based on the culturally prescribed roles of female superiority and male-chivalry, a combination more generally referred to as romantic love. This is our modern understanding of marriage.

During the time this marriage has existed, laws have evolved to buttress and enforce it, laws tilted almost exclusively to favor wives both during the marriage, and especially in the case of its downfall.

As a social construct gynomarriage has not been around forever, with other periods in history generating different forms of marriage as was outlined by August (eg. *Andromarriage* – male centered). During the last 800 years however, and ongoing today, gynomarriage has ruled; so that's what we'll concern ourselves with in this article. To better understand it, let's contrast it with another, far more important 'marriage' holding relevance today.

Biomarriage

Biomarriage (biology + marriage) is a very different idea involving not cultural constructs, but biological necessities built into our DNA. The 'marriage' urged by biology is based on three factors: sexual pleasure; intimate bonding/attachment; and reproduction with the concomitant parenting instinct (hence why both males and females are triggered by neoteny).

Each of these imperatives has operated since our remote hominid past and will continue to compel our behavior for long after gynocentric culture ceases to exist. Like gynomarriage, *biomarriage* takes place between two adults, but in this case has done so for literally millions of years, not hundreds.

I'd like to spend the remainder of this piece talking about *biomarriage* because *gynomarriage* belongs, as any MGTOW or MHRA worth the name will tell you, in the scrap bin of history. People can easily get by without it, but the same cannot be said about *biomarriage* because the compulsion for human bonding, affection, and sex are far too powerful to ignore.

Some MGTOW will refuse to consider a biomarriage with a woman, a serious but otherwise rational choice to make in an environment that exposes men to being savaged by the in-creep of gynocentric exploitation.

If a man refuses the possibility of a non-gynocentric relationship with a woman, what is required are, at bare minimum, artificial avenues for expressing his biological compulsions. He can satisfy sexual needs with porn, imagination, prostitutes, fleshlights or fuck-buddies. He can satisfy his attachment needs at least partially with close friends, family, or perhaps with a pet. Likewise he can satisfy parental instincts via fathering the young among us — teaching school children, working in a daycare center, caring for the disabled, mentoring a fatherless child, coaching little league, looking after orphaned animals, or buying a puppy.

Are these replacement measures enough? Yes, they meet the minimum standard for maintaining physical and emotional stability. But it requires a strong understanding of one's biological needs, and awareness, and a willingness to work hard on meeting those needs. Rather than satisfying our biological needs via "an intimate association or union" we can use a bricolage of band-aids to ensure our biological and psychological health.

Summary

So while you may legitimately think you can reject, nay should reject gynomarriage, do not rush to reject the elements we have detailed under the heading *biomarriage* unless you want to risk your health, and life.

We need to realize that while history has been full of amazing men who never married and eschewed relationships with women, and no man should be shamed for taking this course, it also pays to remind men that choosing isolation from the opposite sex has a cost, and should not be viewed as something trivial to do to yourself. Depression, anxiety, paranoia, delusions, suicide, and more must be protected against. Most people can probably do it, but they'll need more than video games and YouTube in the long run to pull it off. It's going to involve things like meditation, consciously working to both acknowledge your urges, and to cater to them in creative ways.

We can employ alternatives to satisfy our biological urges, but we might also revisit the question of whether there's a way to conduct a biomarriage with a real flesh-n-blood human being minus the gynocentrism – think of it as a biofriendship based on the more essential facts of human being. I'd like to think that's possible, if not now then sometime in the future.

PART FOUR

The Status Quo

17. What Happened to Chivalry?

I have a Google alert for the word chivalry, and not a day goes by that I don't receive several articles on the topic. The articles appear slightly tilted toward the theme 'Male chivalry is dead,' followed by a reasonable number demonstrating 'Chivalry is alive and well' – the latter because some man, somewhere, risked life, limb or money to serve a woman's immediate welfare.

To be sure, chivalry displayed by individual men is on the decline, and women, men, government and mainstream media denounce this devolution with one voice: Men are becoming selfish pigs. MRAs and MGTOW choose to summarize it differently; that men are sick of being exploited and have chosen to shed their unnecessary selflessness.

Chivalry is documented in etiquette manuals of prior centuries explaining how a man is to take off his hat in a woman's presence, shake her hand, open doors, buy her gifts, and assist her in a multitude of ways. The message in these gestures is deference to the superiority of females:

> "If you see a lady whom you do not know, unattended, and wanting the assistance of a man, offer your services to her *immediately*. Do it with great courtesy, taking off your hat and begging the honour of assisting her." [Gynocentric etiquette for men – 1847]

> "In the familiar intercourse of society, a well-bred man will be known by the delicacy and deference with which he behaves towards females. That man would deservedly be looked upon as very deficient in proper respect and feeling, who should take any physical advantage of one of the weaker sex, or offer any personal slight towards her. Woman looks, and properly looks, for protection to man. It is the province of the husband to shield the wife from injury; of the father to protect the daughter; the brother has the same duty to perform towards the

sister; and, in general, every man should, in this sense, be the champion and the lover of every woman. Not only should he be ready to protect, but desirous to please, and willing to sacrifice much of his own personal ease and comfort, if, by doing so, he can increase those of any female in whose company he may find himself. Putting these principles into practice, a well-bred man, in his own house, will be kind and respectful in his behaviour to every female of the family. He will not use towards them harsh language, even if called upon to express dissatisfaction with their conduct. In conversation, he will abstain from every allusion which would put modesty to the blush. He will, as much as in his power, lighten their labors by cheerful and voluntary assistance. He will yield to them every little advantage which may occur in the regular routine of domestic life:—the most comfortable seat, if there be a difference; the warmest position by the winter's fireside; the nicest slice from the family joint, and so on." [Gynocentric etiquette for men – 1873]

"It must always be borne in mind that the assumption of Woman's social superiority lies at the root of these rules of conduct." [Gynocentric etiquette for men – 1897]

One reason for a decline of male chivalry is the vanishing payoff. Women no longer reciprocate for chivalry via good ol fashioned gestures like cooking, homemaking, praise, and affection that would have occurred at the time the above comments were penned. Today they don't even receive a thank you… is it any wonder men are seeing chivalry as a bad deal? The meal ticket, the flowers, the slaving at a job, the deference is all better spent on oneself.

Despite the hand-wringing over a decline in chivalry, women appear to be doing very well for themselves; they are well decked out with material goods, they display increasing body-freedom and body-pride, and their entry into workplace and careers is unprecedented. Society continues to indulge them as much as it ever did – *more*.

With this bare fact one might ask if chivalry merely *appears* to be on the decline and if women are receiving it from another source? My observation – obvious to many in the manosphere – is that they have corralled a rich new source of chivalry.

From Husband Sam to Uncle Sam

The heading is from Dr, Warren Farrell's *Myth of Male Power*, where he describes how men have traditionally striven to institute women-centered government by acting as women's proxy agents in the political sphere. This behavior, explains Farrell, is based on the chivalrous tradition of male servicing of women's needs. The following passage from Farrell's book explains the phenomenon:

> "Doesn't the fact that almost all legislators are men prove that men are in charge and can choose when to and when not to look out for women's interests? Theoretically, yes. But practically speaking the American legal system cannot be separated from the voter. And in the 1992 Presidential election , 54 percent of the voters were female, 46 percent were male. (Women's votes outnumber men's by more than 7 million). Overall, a legislator is to a voter what a chauffeur is to the employer – both look like they're in charge but both can be fired if they don't go where they're told. When legislators do not appear to be protecting women, it is almost always because women differ on what constitutes protection. (For example, women voted almost equally for Republicans and Democrats during the combination of the four presidential elections prior to Clinton).

> "The Government as Substitute Husband did for women what labor unions still have not accomplished for men. And men pay dues for labor unions; the taxpayer pays the dues for feminism. Feminism and government soon become taxpayer-supported women's unions. The political parties have become like two parents in a custody battle, each vying for their daughter's love by promising to do the most for her. How destructive to women is this? We have restricted humans from giving "free" food to bears and dolphins because we know that such feeding would make them dependent and lead to their extinction. But when it comes to our own species, we have difficulty seeing the

connection between short-term kindness and long-term cruelty: we give women money to have more children, making them more dependent with each child and discouraging them from developing the tools to fend for themselves. The real discrimination against women, then, is "free feeding."

Ironically, when political parties or parents compete for females' love by competing to give it, the result is not gratitude but entitlement. And the result should not be gratitude, because the political party, like the needy parent, becomes unconsciously dependent on keeping the female dependent. Which turns the female into "the other" — the person given to, not the equal participant. In the process, it fails to do what is every parent's and every political party's job — to raise an adult, not maintain a child.

But here's the rub. When the entitled child has the majority of the votes, the issue is no longer whether we have a patriarchy or a matriarchy — we get a victimarchy. And the female-as-child genuinely feels like a victim because she never learns how to obtain for herself everything she learns to expect. Well, she learns how to obtain it for herself by saying "it's a woman's right" — but she doesn't feel the mastery that comes with a lifetime of doing it for herself. And even when a quota includes her in the decision-making process, she still feels angry at the "male dominated government" because she feels both the condescension of being given "equality" and the contradiction of being given equality. She is still "the other." So, with the majority of the votes, she is both controlling the system and angry at the system." [The Myth of Male Power]

Do we need further evidence of "what ever happened to chivalry?" Not only have politicians taken over the job of chivalric appeasement of the ladies, it appears both the Left and Right of politics are jousting each other for the privilege to serve them. This I can understand… how else might they get elected?

John Stuart Mill, champion of feminism, urged shifting of the responsibility for chivalry out of the hands of every man and into the legislative framework of government proper, contending that chivalry was not always reliable and must give way to a more reliable, State-enforced protection and benevolence toward women. He writes:

> "From the combination of the two kinds of moral influence thus exercised by women, arose the spirit of chivalry: the peculiarity of which is to aim at combining the highest standard of the warlike qualities with the cultivation of a totally different class of virtues – those of gentleness, generosity, and self-abnegation towards the non-military and defenseless classes generally, and a special submission and worship directed towards women; who were distinguished from the other defenceless classes by the high rewards which they had it in their power voluntarily to bestow on those who endeavoured to earn their favour, instead of extorting their subjection...
>
> The main foundations of the moral life of modern times must be justice and prudence; the respect of each for the rights of every other, and the ability of each to take care of himself. Chivalry left without legal check all those forms of wrong which reigned unpunished throughout society; it only encouraged a few to do right in preference to wrong, by the direction it gave to the instruments of praise and admiration. But the real dependence of morality must always be upon its penal sanctions – its power to deter from evil. The security of society cannot rest on merely rendering honour to right, a motive so comparatively weak in all but a few, and which on very many does not operate at all." [J. S. Mill: The Subjection of Women – 1869]

Ernest B. Bax confirms that the chivalric behavior of both Left and Right of politics was indeed, per Mill's suggestion, well underway by the year 1907:

> "All parties, all sorts and conditions of politicians, from the fashionable and Conservative west-end philanthropist to the Radical working-men's clubbite, seem (or seemed until lately) to have come to an unanimous conclusion on one point – to

wit, that the female sex is grievously groaning under the weight of male oppression." [Essays: New & Old (1907), pp.108-119]

Feminism draws its strength from chivalry, but instead of soliciting chivalry from men in the traditional, interpersonal manner it has learned how to get it solely from the government – holding the government to ransom thanks to suffragettes gaining the vote for ~~gynocentrism~~ women.

Instead of men giving up seats in buses, government now provides seats in legislative assemblies and boardrooms via quotas. Instead of men opening car doors for women, government opens doors into universities and workforces via affirmative action. Instead of men being the sole protectors of women from violence, government now protects them with an army of police specially trained to service women's accusations (over and above more serious crimes). Instead of men providing living expenses, governments now provide it as social welfare and compensation for the 'wage gap'. Etc. ….. government as substitute husband.

All this compliments of feminism's pressuring the Left and Right into chivalric leadership. The only difference between the two sides of politics is that the Left is more sycophantic in its deliverance of chivalric rule – and the Right more heroic in its deliverance of chivalry. Same gynocentrism, different knight.

Gynocentric chivalry was an unbalanced idea to begin with. Men are now backing away from the custom, and we can yearn for the day government on both sides on the political fence does the same. Perhaps when the world's growing army of grass eaters brings about a collapse in revenue they will see the light. In the meantime, let's not give feminists a pass on their claim to have walked away from chivalry…. they have merely found a new source.

18. Feminism – The Same Old Story

Before being given the name feminism, the obsession with women's status was referred to as the *Querelle des Femmes* or quarrel about women. The *querelle* consisted of a perpetual social movement that used damseling to call for more chivalry and more courtly love, a move which ultimately afforded women more power.

These three elements of gynocentrism first born in medieval Europe – damseling, chivalry and courtly love – continue to serve as the driver of the modern feminism. Indeed feminism today is little more, and little less, than a perpetuation of this medieval triad, providing its internal drive even as individual feminists disavow these essentials with rhetorical obfuscations.

With this charge in mind let's revisit the holy trinity above with a focus on behaviors central to modern feminism.

Damseling or "victim feminism"

Most observers today, including feminist observers like Christina Hoff-Sommers, Camille Paglia, Rene Denfeld, Katie Roiphe and others agree that feminism comes close, if not all the way, to being a cult of victimhood.

The phenomenon has variously been referred to as grievance feminism, victim feminism, safe space feminism, and even fainting-couch feminism – with Christina Hoff-Sommers portraying its mythos as "a battle between fragile maidens and evil predators." [1]

Feminist icon Naomi Wolf tells that victim feminism evolved out of "old habits of ladylike behavior that were cloaked in the guise of radicalism," [2] and laments that a substantial segment of modern feminism is devoted to its cause.

Denfeld writes that current feminists "promote a new status for women: that of the victim," and adds:

> "This is victim mythology. From rape redefinitions to feminist theory on the "patriarchy," victimization has become the subtext of the movement, the moral to be found in every feminist story. Together these stories form a feminist mythology in which a singular female subject is created: woman as a helpless, violated, and oppressed victim. Victim mythology says that men will always be predators and women will always be their prey. It is a small place to live, a place that tells women that there is really no way out.
>
> "Like other mythologies, victim mythology reduces the complexity of human interaction to grossly oversimplified mythical tales, a one-note song, where the message of the story becomes so important that fiction not only triumphs over fact but the realities of women's experiences are dismissed and derided when they conflict with the accepted female image.[3]

While Denfeld does a good job of describing feminism's victim mentality, she labors under a myth of her own by characterizing such behaviour as a "new" fetish among feminists. Anyone reading through the history of feminist literature can see it appealed to by literally every feminist writer. Even a century ago Ernest Belfort Bax was able to say that feminists "do their best to bluff their dupes by posing as the victims of a non-existent male oppression."[4]

> Feminists well know that the most grotesquely far-fetched cry about the injustice of man to woman will meet with a ready ear. They well know that they get here fond and foolish man on his soft side. Looking at the matter impartially, it is quite evident that man's treatment of woman is the least vulnerable point in his moral record. Woman, as such, he has always treated with comparative generosity. But it is, of course, to the interests of the abettors of female domination to pretend the contrary. Accordingly everything has been done to excite prejudice in favour of woman as the innocent and guileless

victim of man's tyranny, and the maudlin Feminist sentiment of the "brute" man has been carefully exploited to this end.[5]

In all of these accounts the behavior being described is *damseling*, a practice feminists have been at the forefront of preserving from the medieval canon. Evoked in conjunction with claims of male brutality, rapiness, depravity and insensitivity, the ultimate purpose of damseling is to draw chivalric responses from men, a routine Wolf makes clear in her remark that "victim feminism casts women as sexually pure and mystically nurturing, and stresses the evil done to these 'good' women as a way to petition for their rights." [6]

A famous example of feminist damseling, both literal and figurative, is Anita Sarkeesian. Sarkeesian is known for raising concerns that video-games are misogynistic – like most everything else found in the feminist worldview. Her primary concern was that female game characters are often portrayed as damsels-in-distress saved by male heroes, which promotes, she says, sexual objectification and a range of other problems. To address that issue in video games she moved to launch a study project to raise awareness.

Sarkeesian established a fundraiser for $6,000.00 for her project, but after receiving some initial trolling by trolls on social media she damseled herself to potential donors by saying she was under grave threat, swooning with such finesse that she was showered with 158K in donations from fellow feminists and white knights. Over a thousand people donated after hearing of her "plight."

With that financial success, Sarkeesian subsequently replayed the scenario over and again particularly in the context of further fundraising efforts and public speaking; swooning about online attacks directed against her or over female gamers enduring abject sexism, female video-game characters being cast in degrading and/or humiliating roles, and about young impressionable girls being robbed of agency after being subjected to the damsel trope in games.

Sarkeesian's case is particularly poignant because, from the many subjects she could have highlighted to damsel herself for attention, she chose to damsel herself over the very existence of damsels. This demonstrates that even when disavowing the medieval pageant of damsels in distress, feminists continue to enact it even while obfuscating their complicity in the tradition.

Feminism would have died out long ago if it were not for the power of this ancient ruse, and while damseling continues to draw rewards from a public primed to cater to it, the planet will increasingly come to resemble a tower full of imprisoned, vulnerable Disney Princesses.

Chivalry – from husband Sam to Uncle Sam

Equity feminist Christina Hoff-Sommers states that men need to be civilized with chivalric manners, a belief outlined in an interview with Emily Esfahani Smith, where she said, "Chivalry is grounded in a fundamental reality that defines the relationship between the sexes," and adding a warning, "If women give up on chivalry, it will be gone." [7]

While feminists like Hoff-Sommers admit their reliance on a sexist version of chivalry, others are less candid about it, going even so far as pretending they don't need chivalry despite their demonstrable appeal to it in most of their activism. Many observers however can see through the anti-chivalry posturing.

Feminism draws its power from chivalric support, but instead of soliciting it from men in the traditional, interpersonal manner it has learned how to get it solely from the government – holding the government to ransom ever since the suffragettes damsaled the vote for women. Since that time politicians have only been too willing to furnish demands by feminists in exchange for voting the candidate into power and allowing him to retain office – and conversely politicians who fail to uphold the chivalric contract are promptly voted out.

The results of this compact are obvious to anyone who looks at political decisions with impartiality.

Instead of men giving up seats in buses, government now provides seats in legislative assemblies and boardrooms via quotas. Instead of men opening car doors for women, government opens doors into universities and workforces via affirmative action. Instead of men being the sole protectors of women from violence, government now protects them with an army of police specially trained to service women's accusations (over and above more serious crimes). Instead of men providing living expenses, governments now provide it as social welfare and compensation for the wage-gap. Government as substitute husband.

The appeal to chivalry is not confined to government institutions alone. The appeal also goes out to sporting clubs, business owners, CEOs and private institutions who respond to the damsel's call with women-only busses, women-only safe spaces, pink car parking spaces with extra lighting and security with male escorts and chaperones, or with feminist adverts at sports venues, sportsmen wearing pink to raise money for all manner of feminist projects, and that on top of monies already heaped at their feet by politicians eager to please.

This is not a recent development; it can be witnessed in mirror image as far back as a century ago. Back then, Bax was able to tie feminism so definitively with the act of chivalry-seeking that he actually labeled the women's liberation movement "chivalry feminism." Moreover, Bax saw through the superficial disavowals;

> The justification for the whole movement of Modern Feminism in one of its main practical aspects – namely, the placing of the female sex in the position of privilege, advantage and immunity – is concentrated in the current conception of "chivalry."

> It is plain then that chivalry as understood in the present day really spells sex privilege and sex favouritism pure and simple, and that any attempts to define the term on a larger basis, or to give it a colourable rationality founded on fact, are simply subterfuges, conscious or unconscious, on the part of those who put them forward…

> Such is "chivalry" as understood to-day – the deprivation, the robbery from men of the most elementary personal rights in order to endow women with privileges at the expense of men.[8]

Chivalry feminism today, same as it ever was, relying on men's generosity to perpetuate its creed of power.

Courtly love as 'Respectful Relationships'

The phrase 'Respectful Relationships' is shorthand for a range of conventions promoted by feminists to govern interactions between men and women, particularly in the context of romantic interactions. The conventions detail acceptable speech and actions in the contexts of socializing, friendship, flirting and sex, emphasizing a man's duty to respect women's emotional comfort, self-esteem, and dignity.

Portrayed overtly as a method of reducing men's abusiveness, the program maintains that even men and boys who do *not* display abusive behaviors should be enculturated in its protocols as a prophylactic, and concomitantly to afford dignity and self-esteem to women. This is where the respectful relationships program moves past the overt goal of reducing violence and into the covert goal of maintaining and increasing the power of women.

As we begin to look at the detail of Respectful Relationship we could almost mistake it for Andreas Capellanus' work *The Art of Courtly Love* where the medieval rules of romance were codified in meticulous prescriptions for male deference, homage, and courtesy toward women. Considering this parallel, the feminist movement appears to have provided a new language for a very old set of sexual customs, essentially reiterating that which has been with us all along.

Central to the art of courtly love was the expectation that men practice *love service* toward women based on a model of vassals or serfs in relation to a feudal lord. That relationship model of serf-to-Lord was adopted wholesale to regulate love relationships whereby women were literally approached as the lord (*midons*) in each male-female encounter. As Medievalist Sandra Alfonsi explains;

> Scholars soon saw striking parallels between feudalistic practices and certain tenets of Courtly Love. The comparisons lie in certain resemblances shared by vassalage and the courtly

"love service." Fundamental to both was the concept of obedience. As a vassal, the liegeman swore obedience to his lord. As a courtly lover, the poet chose a lady to whom he was required to swear obedience. Humility and obedience were two concepts familiar to medieval man, active components of his Weltanschauung...

> The entire concept of love-service was patterned after the vassal's oath to serve his lord with loyalty, tenacity, and courage. These same virtues were demanded of the poet. Like the liegeman vis-a-vis his sovereign, the poet approached his lady with fear and respect. Submitted to her, obedient to her will, he awaited a fief or honor as did the vassal. His compensation took many forms: the pleasure of his lady's company in her chamber or in the garden; an avowal of her love; a secret meeting; a kiss or even le surplus, complete unity. Like the lord, the woman who was venerated and served was expected to reward her faithful and humble servant.[9]

The idea behind love service was that men should demonstrate the quality of their commitment to women; was it merely lust or obedient and sacrificial love? If the woman decided it was "love" then she might decide to engage more intimately with him, as Joseph Campbell explains:

> "The woman is looking for authenticity in a relationship, so she delays *merci* until she is guaranteed that this man who is proposing himself to her is one of a gentle heart... And, the women were in control, that's all there is to it. The man is the one who is advancing, the one performing the acts of guarding bridges, or whatever bit of foolishness she puts on him, but, she's in control. And her problem is to live in a relationship that is authentic of love, and the only way she can do it is by testing the one who offers himself. She isn't offering herself, he's offering himself. But, she's in control of what happens then with step two.[10]

> "The technical term for a woman's granting of herself was *merci*; the woman grants her merci. Now, that might consist in

her permission for the man to kiss her on the back of the neck once every Whitsuntide, you know, something like that – or it may be a full giving in love. That would depend upon her estimation of the character of the candidate. The essential idea was to test this man to make sure that he would suffer things for love, and that this was not just lust.

The tests that were given then by women involved, for example, sending a chap out to guard a bridge. The traffic in the Middle Ages was somewhat encumbered by these youths guarding bridges. But also the tests included going into battle. A woman who was too ruthless in asking her lover to risk a real death before she would acquiesce in anything was considered sauvage or "savage". Also, the woman who gave herself without the testing was "savage". There was a very nice psychological estimation game going on here.[11]

Today that psychological estimation game (as Campbell puts it) might involve asking consent to sit with a woman, appealing politely for a date, waiting patiently for her to call or sweep right, keeping his knees together to avoid manspreading, or asking for permission to speak in order to prove he is not talking over her or mansplaining. Such demonstrations show the feminist woman that he has a gentle heart, and that he is willing to suffer things for love.

That psychological testing also encompasses public activities which demonstrate a man's commitment to serving womankind as a whole. Examples would be a man walking a mile in her shoes, or joining White Ribbon Campaigns that require men, as was required of the medieval knights, to pledge oaths to "Never to condone, or remain silent about violence towards women and girls" and especially to intervene when learning of any male behaving offensively toward a woman.

Today's White Ribbon "oath" bears a striking resemblance to the 14th century enterprise of the Green Shield with the White Lady (*Emprise de l'Escu vert à la Dame Blanche*) in which men committed themselves for the duration of five years to serving women. Inspired by the ideal of courtly love, the stated purpose of the order was to guard and defend the honor, estate, goods, reputation, fame and praise of all ladies. It was an undertaking that earned the praise of protofeminist Christine de Pizan. The continuity of chivalry and courtly love from the medieval knightly oath to the modern feminist-inspired oath is remarkable in its consistency.

In line with most women who expect men to follow medieval rules of love concerning male courtesy, the feminist movement is geared toward enforcing the same goal. Feminism however *postures* itself as disavowing that goal even while they are at the forefront of institutionalizing it in our families, our schools, our political structures and laws.

Each of the psychological tests mentioned above are evidence of a *love service* called for by feminist activists. Or worded differently, they are sanctified methods by which men are called to demonstrate obedience and a 'gentle heart' in contrast to the brutality, rapiness and exploitativeness of the savage heart; the default feminist conception of men.

I will close here with the words of an academic feminist, one not so coy about identifying courtly love with the project of feminism. Elizabeth Reid Boyd of the School of Psychology and Social Science at Edith Cowan University, and Director of the Centre for Research for Women in Western Australia with more than a decade as a feminist researcher and teacher of women's studies tells:

> In this article I muse upon arguments that romance is a form of feminism. Going back to its history in the Middle Ages and its invention by noblewomen who created the notion of courtly love, examining its contemporary popular explosion and the concurrent rise of popular romance studies in the academy that has emerged in the wake of women's studies, and positing an empowering female future for the genre, I propose that reading and writing romantic fiction is not only personal escapism, but also political activism.
>
> Romance has a feminist past that belies its ostensible frivolity. Romance, as most true romantics know, began in medieval

times. The word originally referred to the language romanz, linked to the French, Italian and Spanish languages in which love stories, songs and ballads were written. Stories, poems and songs written in this language were called romances to separate them from more serious literature – a distinction we still have today. Romances were popular and fashionable. Love songs and stories, like those of Lancelot and Guinevere, Tristan and Isolde, were soon on the lips of troubadours and minstrels all over Europe. Romance spread rapidly. It has been called the first form of feminism (Putnam 1970).[12]

Reid Boyd finishes her paper by waxing poetic about the many joys of romantic love, and of its increasing popularity in academe.

Same as it ever was, the project of modern feminism can be summarized as championing victimhood (damseling), soliciting favors from men and governments (chivalry), and promoting "respectful" relationships by men-toward-women (courtly love).

References:

[1] Christina Hoff-Sommers, *How fainting couch feminism threatens freedom*, American Enterprise Institute 2015
[2] Naomi Wolf, *Fire With Fire: New Female Power*, 1993
[3] Rene Denfeld, *The New Victorians: A Young Woman's Challenge to the Old Feminist Order*, 1995
[4] Ernest B. Bax, *Feminism and Female Suffrage*, 1910
[5] Ernest B. Bax, *Mr. Belfort Bax Replies to his Feminist Critics*, 1908
[6] Naomi Wolf, *Fire With Fire: New Female Power*, 1993
[7] Emily Esfahani Smith, *Let's Give Chivalry Another Chance,* The Atlantic, Dec 10 2012
[8] Ernest B. Bax, Chapter-5 'The Chivalry Fake' in *The Fraud of Feminism*, 1913
[9] Sandra Alfonsi, *Masculine Submission in Troubadour Lyric*, 1986
[10] Joseph Campbell, *Parzival, the Graal, and Grail Legends*, talk at the Ojai Foundation, 1987
[11] Joseph Campbell, *The Power of Myth*, interview with Bill Moyers, 1988

[12] Elizabeth Reid Boyd, *Romancing Feminism: From Women's Studies to Women's Fiction*, 2014

19. Gynocentrism: Why So Hard To Kill?

Many theories exist as to why we are saddled with a gynocentric culture in which men, to put it simplistically, play the role of servant to women. The explanation people choose will determine whether they believe gynocentrism is a permanent or temporary fact of human existence, and will dictate how they are likely to respond to it.

The first explanation is one of biological determinism – that men have always kowtowed to women regardless of fluctuations in cultural habits, customs, taboos and beliefs. Our genes, according to this theory, make men little more than nerve reflexes primed to obtain sex with females and reproduce – that we must position ourselves as slaves in order to meet that end.

A more reasonable version of the biology hypothesis was proposed by Lester F. Ward in his "Gynæcocentric theory"[1] which frames women as the dominant sex by dint of biology. Evolutionary Psychologists and Difference Feminists, who often collaborate,[2] support this view via anthropological, zoological and other scientific evidence. The basic theory holds that in the underpopulated world of the past, wombs were a precious and key resource to human survival, hence a genetic predisposition toward gynocentrism was a survival advantage. With the current overpopulation, however, wombs are now plentiful and cheap but our biological predispositions still make us overvalue them – ie. a redundant gynocentrism is built into our nervous system at a time when overpopulation could wipe out our species.

Biological determinists conclude that extreme gynocentrism is a permanent feature of human existence, and thus abandoning interactions with women is the only viable option if men want to be free of it: we must drop out of male-female interactions in order to avoid inbuilt gynocentric reflexes.

A completely different explanation is that gynocentrism is an extreme *cultural* exaggeration of human potential, one that hasn't played constantly throughout human history. This explanation leaves open the option to confront and potentially change gynocentric culture in the knowledge that it is not an inevitable fate for men to suffer.

The two perspectives above, one theory placing the accent on biology and the other on culture, have serious ramifications for how men conceptualize and responded to the problem – the one abandoning it, the other rejecting it and posing an alternative approach to male-female relations.

I personally wager that extreme gynocentrism, that which is based on chivalry and romantic love, is a novelty in the long walk of human evolution. And yet it doesn't appear to be going away, at least not quickly, despite concerted efforts to dismantle it. What could be going on?

Why is gynocentrism still alive?

With the different approaches to understanding gynocentrism touched on, I'd like to use the rest of this article to deal with one question – how to destroy the beast.

I'd like to think it will come to an end through natural processes. Human beings possess inbuilt regulating mechanisms that work to achieve homeostasis in biological, psychological and social systems, and which tend to cull extreme behaviors when they interfere with the overall psycho-biological economy.

Gynocentrism is an example of an extreme, discord-creating behavior, and yet those innate balancing mechanisms do not seem to be culling it from our repertoire. Why is that?

One explanation is that media is censoring those voices calling, nay *yelling*, for homeostasis.

Everyone draws information from the environment, and especially from the media, to construct internal schemas of the external world.

We create internal pictures of how things work. However, if the environment is not providing adequate data, or worse, something in the environment is actively *censoring* the available data, it severely weakens our ability to understand the world and to create a balanced way of moving through it.

Censorship of the media by gynocentrists is not new, but historically speaking appears to be the No.1 force blocking a change in gender culture.

Go back 200 years and newspapers were the dominant media which began with some remarkable examples of free speech. But as soon as criticism of gynocentrism increased, the censor army infiltrated – free speech in newspapers was crushed. Ernest B. Bax for example wrote;

> When, however, the bluff is exposed… then the apostles of feminism, male and female, being unable to make even a plausible case out in reply, resort to the boycott, and by ignoring what they cannot answer, seek to stop the spread of the unpleasant truth so dangerous to their cause. The pressure put upon publishers and editors by the influential Feminist sisterhood is well known.[3]

And;

> All parties, all sorts and conditions of politicians, from the fashionable and Conservative west-end philanthropist to the Radical working-men's clubbite, seem (or seemed until lately) to have come to an unanimous conclusion on one point – to wit, that the female sex is grievously groaning under the weight of male oppression. Editors of newspapers, keen to scent out every drift of public fancy with the object of regaling their "constant readers" with what is tickling to their palates, will greedily print, in prominent positions and in large type letters expressive of the view in question, whilst they will boycott or, at best, publish in obscure corners any communication that ventures to criticise the popular theory or that adduces facts that tell against it. Were I to pen an impassioned diatribe, tending to prove the villainy of man towards woman, and

painting in glowing terms the poor, weak victim of his despotism, my description would be received with sympathetic approval. Not so, I fear, my simple statement of the unvarnished truth.[4]

Later came TV, which dethroned the old tabloid censorship. The Federal Communications Commission (USA) began handing out broadcasting licenses in the early 1950s (with the highest concentration of license grants and station sign-ons occurring between 1953 and 1956), spurring an explosion of growth in the medium. Half of all U.S. households had television sets by 1955.[5] With that advent, consider the success of Martin Luther King's civil rights campaigning which spanned from 1955 (Montgomery Bus Boycott) through to the mid 1960s. Without TV it would not have happened. Unfortunately, forces of political correctness infiltrated public broadcasting too, applying censorship and eventually dominating TV culture completely.

In the 1990's the new medium of the internet appeared and dethroned the old TV media with its censorship. This opened the door to thousands of revolutions gaining a voice, including the MRM & MGTOW, which have gained traction as cultural forces. But as usual, the cycle of → 1. New media technology → 2. subsequent cultural revolutions, and → 3. eventual feminist censorship, is playing out on the internet….. and we are entering the censorship phase of the cycle.

Those who say feminists will never succeed in censoring the internet are dreaming, and dare I say blind. It's happening – Twitter, Facebook, Youtube, Wikipedia, etc. all being taken over by feminist sensibilities and regulations. Free speech is experiencing a decline on most social media platforms.

The only avenue left is to grab our own domains and websites from which we can enjoy free speech, and to do it NOW before government regulators ask domain providers, hosting companies, and ISPs to institute onerous application criteria for the privilege. In short, give up on Youtube (etc) and grab a domain and website while you still can – social media is dying from censorship, and MGTOW, MRA and outspoken gamers etc will be its first casualties.

Despite the doom and gloom about impending censorship it's not all bad news, *far from it*. The window opened by the internet has been seized upon and used to maximum effect. We have inserted a narrative on what gynocentrism is, what men's issues are, and they've enjoyed considerable reach into the culture. Witness any comments section under an MSM article to gauge the new awareness of -and support for- these same issues. And the narrative is growing…

MHRAs, MGTOW, gamers, PUAs, antifeminists, and a growing coalition of everyday Joes, are poised to drive the nail deeper. We can continue to use social media -in spite of restrictive feminist guidelines- to drive the narrative home : gynocentrism is toxic and we want to to end. And those smart enough to grab their own domains and websites can come down harder with the message knowing there is no Hall Monitor to control our private soapboxes, at least not yet.

In fact let's grow our private websites exponentially so they overshadow PC social media outlets and continue competing with them in the battle for cultural real estate.

This article began with a description of different ways of conceptualizing the origins of gynocentric culture, and the question was posed of why does gynocentrism continue to exist. We then looked at the transformations of mainstream media through recent centuries, noting how media is a double-edged sword, at times championing free speech, and at times censoring it, with the latter being a potential cause for gynocentrism's longevity. Lastly was underlined how the internet currently gives voice to long suppressed thoughts, and of the need to make hay while the sun still shines – i.e. hopefully to make it shine longer and brighter. As long as we keep adding our story to mainstream media, *and being the media*, gynocentrism will atrophy and homeostasis will come.

References:

[1] Lester Frank Ward, *Pure Sociology*, (The gynæcocentric theory, pp. 296-376), published 1903.
[2] For examples of the growing marriage between Evopsychology and difference-feminism, see:

—— David Buss, *Sex, Power, Conflict : Evolutionary and Feminist Perspectives*
—— M. Fisher, J. Garcia, R. chang, *Evolution's Empress: Darwinian Perspectives on the Nature of Women*
[3] Ernest Belfort Bax, The Fraud of Feminism, pp.1-2, published 1913
[4] Ernest Belfort Bax, Essays in Socialism New & Old, pp.108-119, published 1907
[5] History of American Television, *Television in the United States*

PART FIVE

Post Gynocentric Relationships

20. Sex and Attachment

Male motivation is tied to sexual reproduction and men are motivated primarily by urges to have sex with a woman, right?

Wrong… it's more complex than that.

As far back as 1941 Scottish psychiatrist Ronald Fairbairn found that the desire for attachment in human beings, in terms of the overall psychobiological economy, is a more important necessity than the desire for sexual pleasure and reproduction.

This scientific finding, not controversial in the field of psychology, presents something of a heretical view to some men's advocates who, by contrast, seem to have come in recent years to believe that males are ultimately wired for sexual reproduction — which, oddly enough, aligns with the misandrist stereotype of "all men ever want is sex" that so many men find insulting and reductive.

Fairbairn's proposition is now many decades old, but his findings heralded a Copernican revolution within the world of psychological research that would culminate in today's attachment sciences; it moved the discussion beyond the reductionist sexual theories of Darwin and Freud and into new areas–more complex, more subtle, more nuanced, and ultimately more human.

The question attachment scientists explored is: why do couples continue to stay with each other years after producing offspring, and indeed sometimes for decades after all sexual activity has ceased in relationships? The answer is because human beings are pair bonders who get more out of attachment than they do out of copulating.

Since Fairbairn, studies have confirmed that humans possess an array of distinct motivational systems each in communication with the surrounding environment. Of those systems two are singled out as particularly powerful in motivating humans to form relationships – the sexual urge (eros), and -separately- the urge to attach. Of these, attachment is quite simply the most important to the continued survival of the individual. This cannot be overstated: attachment is the more important to individual survival.

As studies reveal, an absence of close and consistent human attachment causes children to literally wither and die, refusing to thrive even when being provided with clothing, food and an adequate number of toys. Children need reliable and consistent relationships in order to thrive. Likewise adults literally sicken both physically and mentally, and often commit suicide, to escape feelings of isolation and loneliness, especially after a relationship breakdown.

A lack of sexual contact on the contrary is not life threatening; you will never see someone die simply because they didn't get to copulate with the opposite sex and reproduce. I would think that seals the case about what is really important to both men and women. Survival of the species depends on sex; survival of the individual depends on the vital bonds of attachment.

What does all this mean to men?

Well, it means that we need to evaluate our attachment needs and our sexual needs separately, and avoid the common mistake of conflating them.

In our psychobiological economy, various desires come into conflict with one another, each jostling for momentary supremacy where one imperative will usurp the claims of another. That game has reached a problematical impasse during the last 800 years because, during that (historically relatively short) time span, human culture has thrown the weight of its patronage into developing, intensifying and enforcing sexual gamesmanship to the degree that our sexual compulsions appear pumped up on steroids and taken to extremes never before seen in the human animal.

If we lived back in Ancient Greece, Rome or anywhere else we would view sex as little more than a bodily function akin to eating and sleeping – an enjoyable but nevertheless basic bodily function without the hype. After the Middle Ages however it developed into a commodity to pimp and trade, and the new cult of sexualized romance that arose resulted in a frustration of our basic need for attachment – a frustration aided and abetted by social institutions placing sexual manipulation at the centre of human interactions.

During these fairly recent centuries of increased hypergamy and sexual focus, our drive to pair-bond continues to shout its demands even while being neglected. Observe for example the not-infrequent feelings of disillusionment and loneliness of serial partner upgraders (hypergamy) or of promiscuous pick-up-artists, or consider the young woman living in her mansion with an aged but wealthy husband to whom she has little or no emotional attachment, and whose loneliness eats away at her sense of contentment despite the trappings of wealth. These examples reveal an urgency surrounding attachment when it is neglected for the sake of secondary sexual or power gains.

Like men, women desire secure attachment beyond whatever sexual advantages they can and do exploit. However, if hypergamous ambitions exist they tend to get in the way and frustrate the powerful need to pair-bond. From the Middle Ages to today we read of men and women bitterly disillusioned by the interference of hypergamy in the desire to form stable pair-bonds. Read for instance the bitter, antifeminist complaints of 12th century Andreas Capellanus or those of 14th century Christine de Pizan, or the disillusionment and ultimate rejection of the benefits of hypergamy in later works like Madam Bovary. These authors knew full well that sexualized romantic love had upset the balance of attachment security for both men and women alike.

The question we should ask ourselves is this: can our human need for attachment be indulged without men and women succumbing to the destructive manipulations of the modern sex code? As men and women opt more for the singles life, rightly rejecting cultural prescriptions for "romance" as bastions of exploitation, have we intellectually thrown out the attachment baby with the exploitation bathwater?

Sexual games need not get in the way of healthy attachment, so why should we live without relationships? Well no one ever said we had to, but in recent years I've sensed a trend both within and without the male-advocacy community (which I've long been part of) that foregoing "relationships" is a necessary part of avoiding sexual manipulation.

This does not seem a prudent attitude to be cultivating, especially in young men who may now be reading men's advocacy websites and making extreme decisions about their lives. Refusing to marry, cohabit, or procreate does not require a cutting off from human society. Even if we don't end up suiciding from loneliness (as so many men do) we need to question if the absence of an intimate relationship can leave us limping, or somehow unfulfilled? Some will say no, and some of these naysayers may well be what are known in attachment science as 'avoidant attachers.' Of those who would say yes, some might recommend we fill our intimacy void with friendships, which is I think a very good starting point. But this leads to a further question of whether there are adequate formulations of friendship that can satisfy our needs in a modern context – a relationship that doesn't rely on the usual corruption at the core of sexualized romantic love.

These questions lead to an exploration of adult human attachment, and modern studies on the subject are abundant from psychological, biological and behavioural points of view. For those interested in following this subject further the Wikipedia entry on Attachment in Adults would be a good place to start, and to branch out from there. Of particular interest is the existence of four basic attachment styles in human beings, indicating that there must also be four main ways of conducting relationships:

Secure attachment (64% of the population)
Anxious–preoccupied attachment (17% of the population)
Fearful–avoidant attachment (12% of the population)
Dismissive–avoidant attachment (7% of the population)*

Only one of these styles (dismissive avoidant) involves a lack of desire for emotionally close relationships (relationships with minimal emotional intimacy may be tolerable to them), while the other three involve a desire to form emotionally intimate attachments. These are biologically-based traits appearing in each man and woman, and they help to account for the behavioural and ideological variability we see among different individuals – for the most part we are working creatively with what's already in our make-up rather than changing our core attachment style.

While some people claim to not need attachment at all, evidence is not in their favour. Thus, for most of us, constructing new ways to form secure relationships with our fellow humans in a rich and rewarding way is an important long-term question, even if we cannot pretend to have all the answers now; we start by knowing what we don't want: relationships of enslavement and entrapment to the opposite sex (or anyone else for that matter) in an environment that makes healthy attachment difficult. But how do we forge a more positive model for human relationships and attachment for ourselves?

We started this essay with an important question: are sex and attachment two relatively different motivations? The answer is a resounding yes! Yes, despite all the pop culture bombardment of sex, sex, sex, the sexual shaming of men, and all the rest, the answer is yes: sex and attachment are not the same. People can live their lives avoiding sexual games but they will not end their lives happily unless they meet their attachment requirements. And while this journey will be different for each person, we must not flinch from seeing the problem for what it is: not "overcoming our urge to procreate," but rather, how to be healthy human beings able to recognize and fulfil our natural need for human intimacy.

Sources

– Frederico Pereira, David E. Scharff, M. D. Fairbairn and Relational Theory (2002)
– Fairbairn, W.R.D., 'Psychoanalytic Studies of the Personality'. (2013)
– Shaver, P.R., Handbook of attachment – Second Edition (2008)
– Shaver, P.R., Attachment in Adulthood: Structure, Dynamics and Change (2010)
* Percentages are a mean average of three randomly selected studies.

Image by LTAL

21. Romantic Love, or Friendship?

> "It is not a lack of love, but a lack of friendship that makes unhappy marriages."
> Friedrich Nietzsche

Modern culture promotes a neurotic vision of what constitutes true love. In the 12th century courtly love served as the basis for a relationship model in which men were to play the role of chivalric vassal to women who assumed the role of an idealised Lady.

C.S. Lewis, back in the middle of the 20th Century, referred to this historical revolution as "the feudalisation of love," and stated that it has left no corner of our ethics, our imagination, or our daily life untouched. "Compared with this revolution," states Lewis, "the Renaissance is a mere ripple on the surface of literature." [1]

Not only has this feudalistic notion of love permeated almost every corner of the globe today, it continues to be vigorously promoted by both feminists and traditionalists alike. The love we are referring to is what Hollywood, romance novels, and other media refer to as "romantic love," the fantasy to which every modern man and woman pledges blind obeisance. Here are two descriptions of romantic love from modern scholars:

C.S. Lewis:

> "Everyone has heard of courtly love, and everyone knows it appeared quite suddenly at the end of the eleventh century at Languedoc. The sentiment, of course, is love, but love of a highly specialized sort, whose characteristics may be enumerated as Humility, Courtesy, and the Religion of Love. The lover is always abject. Obedience to his lady's lightest wish, however whimsical, and silent acquiescence in her

rebukes, however unjust, are the only virtues he dares to claim. Here is a service of love closely modelled on the service which a feudal vassal owes to his lord. The lover is the lady's 'man'. He addresses her as *midons*, which etymologically represents not 'my lady' but 'my lord'. The whole attitude has been rightly described as 'a feudalisation of love'. This solemn amatory ritual is felt to be part and parcel of the courtly life."[2]

C.S. Lewis wrote that many decades ago; I'm not sure "everyone" knows it today. We ought to remember his words, because in the long sweep of human history, what we think has been with us forever is something people only a few generations ago knew to be mostly an artificial, idealized notion.

Slavoj Zizek:

"The knight's relationship to the Lady is thus the relationship of the subject-bondsman, the vassal, to his feudal Master-Sovereign who subjects him to senseless, outrageous, impossible, arbitrary, capricious ordeals. It is precisely in order to emphasize the non-spiritual nature of these ordeals that Lacan quotes a poem about a Lady who demanded that her servant literally lick her arse: the poem consists of the poet's complaints about the bad smells that await him down there (one knows the sad state of personal hygiene in the Middle Ages), and about the imminent danger that, as he is fulfilling his 'duty', the Lady will urinate on his head." [3]

Feminism's mission today is largely the promulgation of this "love," and it is right that men and women learn to reject it, as Men Going Their Own Way (MGTOW), Women Against Feminism (WAF), and Men's Human Rights Advocates (MHRAs) are doing. It is a "love" that dehumanizes males by turning them into masochistic servants, while simultaneously dehumanizing women by idealizing them to the extent that their humanity is obliterated and replaced with an image of divinity. It's a recipe for disaster on both sides; the occasional lucky couple for whom this works is about as rare as a lightning strike, with no evidence that even that lucky few are really happier or more productive than anyone else.

When I consider this disastrous state of affairs that has lead men to boycott relationships, a few questions arise; are we being too rash in our rush from love, and if yes is there a better model, a new model, or perhaps an older model for relationships that we have forgot?

The field of attachment science concludes that an absence of close and consistent human attachment causes children to literally wither and die, refusing to thrive despite being provided with clothing, food and an adequate number of toys. Likewise adults literally commit suicide to escape feelings of isolation and loneliness, especially after a relationship separation. Even if we don't end up suiciding from loneliness we have to ask ourselves if the absence of an intimate relationship in our lives leaves us limping, or somehow unfulfilled? Some would suggest we can fill our intimacy void with friendships, but this leads to a further question of whether there is an adequate formulation of friendship that can satisfy our needs – a relationship that doesn't rely on the usual vassal and lord model at the core of romantic love.

In ancient cultures friendship was a more lofty aspiration than it is today. It was synonymous with love and it often involved sexual intimacy. In Ancient Greek, the same word was used for friend and lover. In our culture we have succeeded in separating friendship from the category we call love, and excised all trace of sex from friendships. Today when we say, "They are just good friends" or "she's only a friend" we are indicating the absence of both intimate love and sex.

To older classical cultures, friendship seemed the happiest and most fully human of the different kinds of loves, and for that reason I wonder whether it's worth reintroducing it here as a guide to relationships between red-pill men and women?

Suppose that rather than running from intimacy we were to demote our idea of "romantic" love from its pedestal, and elevate friendship-love in its place. Suppose also that we steal back sexual attraction and sexual intercourse from the neurotic clutches of "romantic" love, and allow it once again to be part and parcel of friendship if and when relationships call for it.

Before we consider elevating friendship as a replacement for romantic love we need first to detail precisely what it is and how it looks in lived experience, and to that end here are three salient points of definition.

Friendship is based on shared interests

Friendship is based entirely on things people have in common, like some shared insight, interest or taste. It might be cooking, sport, religion, politics, sex, or gardening, and in the best friendships there occurs a handsome combination of these. No friendship can arise without shared interests, because there would be nothing for the friendship to be *about*. Furthermore, that "something" is generally located *outside* oneself and one's relationship – at the football stadium, church, chess-board, or stamp collection. Friendship differs in this respect markedly from "romantic" love in which couples perpetually focus on each other and talk to each other about their love.

Friends hardly ever talk about their friendship. C.S. Lewis captures this with his remark that friends stand side-by-side rather than face-to-face:

> "Friends are not primarily absorbed in each other. It is when we are doing things together that friendship springs up – painting, sailing ships, praying, philosophizing, fighting shoulder to shoulder. Friends look in the same direction. Lovers look at each other – that is, in opposite directions."[1]

This kind of friendship, this *love*, is not something we can have with anyone we meet. We can no more choose in advance who we are going to be close friends with than we can choose what sort of skin colour we are going to be born with. Friendship arises organically when we discover that a previously casual acquaintance, or perhaps a new person we meet, shares significant interests with us; "What? You too? I thought I was the only one!" The pleasure derived from cooperation in that shared interest, and of getting to know them through that activity, provides an avenue for deep bonding and human attachment.

Friendship is based in personal authenticity

Friendship is based on true identities and interests, not on some narrow and dehumanising role we might play. Friendship invites you to speak out about your interests in order to find potential areas of commonality. This is not allowed in so-called "romantic" love lest your interests threaten the narrow feudalistic fantasy. In "romantic" love the main "shared interest" is that script which insists the man play the role of masochistic utility, and the woman an idealised goddess. It is an objectification of both parties.

Friendship is not based on the feudal model: not vassals and overlords, but partners in crime.

Friendship is highly compatible with sex

Sex does not belong to romantic love – it belongs anywhere you want it to belong. Modern culture has begrudgingly allowed for this possibility under the risqué concept of "friends with benefits," but to the ancients it was not daring at all, it was perfectly normal. Friendship also allows for a kind of quasi-romance–or dare I say, a possibly more authentic romance? Have you not had a good friend give you a gift, take you out for a meal, or to the movies? Sex and romantic gestures need not remain colonised by feudalistic notions of romantic love alone.

Sexual attraction and desire also need to be put in their place. They may generate some chemistry and may be the first thing that attracts you to a person, but like the shiny trinket that catches your eye at the shopping mall, you will first stare at it in wonder, maybe have a feel, and then decide whether you really want to take that thing home and share your life with it. Friendship is much the same, and if a person you meet has little in common you will be inclined to leave them on the shelf and move on, despite their sexual attractiveness.

Romantic-love and friendship-love are clearly opposed relationships with opposing motives. A woman might say: "I don't want to be friends with my husband because it will take all the drama and intensity out of our marriage." That is true enough, friendship does take some of the neurotic drama and intensity out of a relationship. But it also takes away the masochism and narcissism, and replaces that sickness with something human and real.

One of the worst-kept secrets about married couples is that they often treat their friends with more kindness, compassion and generosity than they ever do for each other. When best friends are together they are charming, engaging, helpful and courteous, but when they return home to their spouses they appear resentful, angry and uncooperative with each other. Hardly ever do we see this pattern reversed, where people are horrible to friends and at their best with their long term romantic love partners.

Friendship-love not only existed throughout the world before "romantic" love was invented, but it remains active in some pockets of culture today – for instance in China and India. Author Robert Johnson, for instance, writes about the presence of friendship between couples in India, recounting a Hindu marriage rite in which the bride and groom make the solemn but hopeful statement, "You will be my best friend."

Johnson goes further, telling that "In a traditional Hindu marriage, a man's commitment to his wife does not depend on his staying 'in love' with her. Since he was never 'in love' in the first place, there is no way he can fall 'out of love'. His relationship to his wife is based on loving her, not on being 'in love' with the ideal he projects onto her. His relationship is not going to collapse because one day he falls 'out of love,' or because he meets another woman who catches his projection. He is committed to a woman and a family, not to a projection."[4]

Friendship-love appeared long before "romantic" love and *it worked*. The "romantic" version of love is full of narcissism, corruption, entitlement and despair, where dreams collapse and lives are shattered. On the other hand go ask the happily married octogenarian couple who their best friend is – they will look at each other and smile knowing the answer has been beside them for sixty years. Our lives, loves and families fare much better when we base them on this very human kind of love called friendship.

With friendship, men and women have an opportunity to truly go their own way while keeping the option of healthy intimate relationships with either sex alive. Having your cake and eating it too. That would be my suggestion of how we might cure the malaise.

I once again note that the breakdown in relations between men and women has been painful, and men have suffered the most in this I would think; in the current socio-political climate, marriage and even cohabitation is like jumping out of an aeroplane with a chute you're not even sure is going to open. And all change can't simply be political. Still, if we are ever to look forward to a cultural change that might make for a new era of improved relations between the sexes, ditching these feudalistic attitudes about "romantic love," and restoring the ancient tradition of seeing intimate friendship being the highest ideal for a relationship, would probably by a major step in the right direction culturally. This will require a shift in the attitudes of men and women alike, but the evidence for this being possible is strong; we've done it before, and we still see it in some cultures today. It's not impossible for human beings to think and act this way. So can we return to a culture where that's the more normal way of thinking? I'd like to believe that possible for us today, or at least in the future.

References

[1] C.S. Lewis, *Friendship*, chapter in The Four Loves, HarperCollins, 1960
[2] C.S. Lewis, *The Allegory of Love*, Oxford University Press, 1936
[3] Slavoj Zizek, *The Metastases of Enjoyment*, Verso Press, 2005
[4] Robert A. Johnson, *Understanding the Psychology of Romantic Love*, HarperCollins, 1983
[5] Robert C. Solomon, *Love: Emotion, Metaphor, Empathy*, Prometheus Books, 1990
[6] Marcus Tullius Cicero, *Cicero's Essays on Old Age and Friendship*, Translation Publishers, 1926

[7] Lorraine S. Pangle, *Aristotle and the Philosophy of Friendship*, Cambridge University Press, 1986

[8] Irving Singer, *The Nature of Love: Plato to Luther*, University of Chicago Press, 1966

[9] Irving Singer, *The Nature of Love: Courtly and Romantic*, MIT Press, 2009

[10] Alan Soble, *Eros, Agape and Philia: Readings in the Philosophy of Love*, Paragon House, 1998

22. Pleasure-Seeking vs. Relationships

Pleasure-seeking and relationships are the two most powerful forces informing societies, families and the inner life of individuals – and they are often pitted against each other, with one dominating at the expense of the other.

Pleasure-seeking as a philosophical enterprise has been around since at least the ancient Greek philosopher Epicurus, and was more fully elaborated in the writings of Sigmund Freud whose "pleasure principle" lays at the base of all psychoanalytic theory; "What decides the purpose of life," writes Freud, "is simply the programme of the pleasure principle."[1]

For Freud the human libido is a pleasure seeking force, and his popularization of this idea gave the project of global capitalism its internal rationale: every individual is an appetite ruthlessly seeking pleasure, a non-stop consumer. The majority of societies and economies around the world are now reliant on this principle in order to perpetuate themselves.

According to Freud, the pleasure principle is:

– backed by instinctual drive
– selfish
– ruthless
– narcissistic
– focused on the individual above relationships

After 100 years of promoting the importance of the pleasure principle, indeed over-promoting it, today we have become devotees at its shrine, promoting ideas like these:

– narcissism
– sense of entitlement

- pick up artistry
- rampant consumerism
- commodification of interpersonal relationships

How are we feeling about all that pleasure – are we enjoying it yet or are we sick of it? Do you want to dial up the hedonism some more, or do you want to join me in questioning the premise?

Despite capitalism's incestuous relationship with the pleasure-principle, a behavior it does more to perpetuate than merely serve, early psychoanalysts began to see problems with it. The problem was not with the idea that humans are pleasure seekers, but that the idea had been afforded far more importance in human behavior than it deserved – there were other more important factors to human being that had been given short shrift.

Like relationships.

Early psychoanalyst Ronald Fairbairn was amongst the first to write about the importance of relationships over pleasure seeking. In 1944 Fairbairn explained the impasse with Freud's theory as follows;

> In a previous paper (1941) I attempted to formulate a new version of the libido theory and to outline the general features which a systematic psychopathology based upon this re-formulation would appear to assume. The basic conception which I advanced on that occasion, and to which I still adhere, is to the effect that libido is primarily object-seeking (rather than pleasure-seeking, as in the classic theory), and that it is to disturbances in the object-relationships of the developing ego that we must look for the ultimate origin of all psychopathological conditions. This conception seems to me not only to be closer in accord with psychological facts and clinical data than that embodied in Freud's original libido theory, but also to represent a logical outcome of the present stage of psychoanalytical thought and a necessary step in the further development of psychoanalytical theory… [2]

This revolution in psychoanalytic thinking launched the school of Object Relations psychology, with the word 'Object' standing for real people we enter into relationships with. Object Relations psychology is based more on attachment theory than on the pleasure principle. In a nutshell this school, which superseded psychoanalysis, is described as:

> Object relations is based on the theory that the primary motivational factors in one's life are based on human relationships, rather than sexual or aggressive triggers. Object relations is a variation of psychoanalytic theory and diverges from Freud's belief that we are pleasure seeking beings; instead it suggests that humans seek relationships.[3]

Has the mental health industry caught up? Yes, I'm pleased to say that portions of the industry have not only caught up, they are driving the research on attachment forward. Other sections of the industry, however, especially those on the front line of offering services, continue to devote undue importance to pleasure-seeking through the advocacy of self-actualization and 'me and my wants.'

The problems of gynocentrism and treating of men as utilities will not be addressed until we look at how these things are used to generate pleasure. One reason we have stalled in relativizing the pleasure-principle and affirming the findings of attachment science, is that it's obviously not in the current society's interest to do so. To catch up and look in the mirror is to die – the whole goddam system collapses – our beliefs, our customs, our financial systems.

But look at it we must, both collectively and individually if we wish to promote mental health.

Do we really need more shopping, drugs, stimulation, sex and food? Frankly many men are done… they've had enough food and sex to last 20 lifetimes. They don't need more pick-up techniques, they don't need more research fads focusing on sexual drives a-la-Freud, and they certainly don't need to consume more – they've consumed quite enough, thank you.

If we insist on believing the pleasure principle is paramount, that it is our most pressing genetic imperative, along with the belief that "all men want is sex" that so many men find annoying, then our only escape is to follow a sick, nihilistic version of retreat from the world. How else to escape the call of pleasure? Our western culture's devotion to the pleasure principle leaves it stuck in an insoluble loop, like a snake devouring itself and not realizing that the tail it is eating is its own.

I say western culture because there are whispers of an alternative in other cultures that, alas are also being corrupted for the newfangled focus on the pleasure principle that drives the mighty dollar. I have listened to people from various Asian countries – Cambodia, China, Thailand – who talk of valuing their relationships and families somewhat more than their own pleasure-seeking ambitions. Watch how they eat together, having several dishes of food on the table that they all share, not everyman for his own narcissistic pleasure. In some of those countries the individual has to wait until vehicles pass before he can cross the road, but in ours we have laws stating that cars must stop in obeisance to the almighty individual and his pleasures. I have also heard some Asians ask, perplexed, why women wear skimpy clothes in winter, not knowing that our cultures are all about inviting consumption and commodification of every person in order to feed each others' predatory pleasures.

None of this is to deny the pleasure principle and its powerful pull on men's lives. But pleasure quickly becomes hedonism without relationship to temper it, and it leads not to a meaningful life but to emptiness and nihilism where 'opting out' is the only response – a response that looks more like a sickness than a cure.

Now what does all this mean to the wellbeing of men? In short, everything. Getting these two vital aspects of human nature in balance is not only the secret to psychological health, but our lives may literally depend on it. Regaining that balance can start with paying more attention to our relationship needs and less to pleasure – more to the girl-next-door and less to the girl with the exaggerated cleavage, boob jobs, and love bombs.

Moreover, the problem does not stop at intimate adult relations, and applies to family as well. If every family member is chasing his or her own pleasures, they are more likely than ever to spin off in their own directions like atoms rapping in a void – there's no glue holding the unit together, no relationship – and custody battles, selfishness and estrangement are the inevitable result: Me and my pleasures first.

To be sure, regular relationships also afford experiences of pleasure or contentment, albeit of lower intensity than the pleasure-seeking described by Freud. Another distinguishing feature is that relationships don't involve the *use* of people in the same ruthless manner as does the pleasure principle – ie. not the same as we experience when devouring food or having sex. Relationship is more concerned with situating oneself in a context and gaining emotional satisfactions from that – from belonging, from being-with-others, as contrasted with using objects to satisfy appetite. A second distinguishing feature of intimate relationships is that the individual has *concern* for the objects of his attachment – whereas the pleasure-seeking appetite has no concern over its use of people nor its destruction of same.

Jungian analyst Robert A. Johnson writes about the two impulses as two kinds of "love." He calls the pleasure-seeking impulse *romantic love*, and the relationship-seeking version *human love*. Here is his description of the two;

> Many years ago a wise friend gave me a name for human love. She called it "stirring-the-oatmeal" love. She was right: Within this phrase, if we will humble ourselves enough to look, is the very essence of what human love is, and it shows us the principal differences between human love and romance. Stirring the oatmeal is a humble act-not exciting or thrilling. But it symbolizes a relatedness that brings love down to earth.
>
> Jung once said that feeling is a matter of the small. And in human love, we can see that it is true. The real relatedness between two people is experienced in the small tasks they do together: the quiet conversation when the day's upheavals are at rest, the soft word of understanding, the daily companionship, the encouragement offered in a difficult

moment, the small gift when least expected, the spontaneous gesture of love. When a couple are genuinely related to each other, they are willing to enter into the whole spectrum of human life together. They transform even the unexciting, difficult, and mundane things into a joyful and fulfilling component of life. By contrast, romantic love can only last so long as a couple are "high" on one another, so long as the money lasts and the entertainments are exciting. "Stirring the oatmeal" means that two people take their love off the airy level of exciting fantasy and convert it into earthy, practical immediacy…

Love is willing to fix breakfast and balance the checkbook. Love is willing to do these "oatmeal" things of life because it is related to a person, not a projection. Human love sees another person as an individual and makes an individualized relationship to him or her.[4]

I outlined the importance of relational attachments in previous chapters Sex and Attachment and Love and friendship. Hopefully these provide some discussion points for new ways to conduct relationships, but more important is asking of the initial question: are we ready to interrogate the pleasure-principle as the foundation of our society?

References:

[1] Sigmund Freud, Civilization, Society and Religion (PFL 12) p. 263 (1991)
[2] Ronald Fairbairn, Psychoanalytic Studies of the Personality pp. 82-83 (1952)
[3] Object Relations, definition from GoodTherapy.org (August 2015)
[4] Robert A. Johnson, We: Understanding the Psychology of Romantic Love, p. 195 (1983

23. Don't Just Do Something, SIT THERE

"To be or not to be- that is the question."
Shakespeare

Being is vital to the health of everyman but is rarely given the consideration it deserves: Being at a cafe, being in nature, being with a friend, being at home, being at peace. Smelling the roses. If allowed, these things have potential to replace some of the incessant *doing* that drives men's existence too early into the coffin.

We've all heard the phrase Women are human beings and men are human doings.[1] It's one of those catchy, hummable lines that everyone agrees with before it slips again from conscious awareness – even as it remains in front of our eyes and in our daily behavior. Even as it slips from awareness the fact remains that *doing* without *being*, and *being* without *doing*, bespeak unbalanced lives, ones that can and do lead to pathology.

The question we need to ask is what are we doing about it? I don't mean what are we doing about it as a movement, but what are we, each of us, doing about it in our own personal lives. While some men are already addressing the balance, others may still be searching for the right balance, and for a better understanding of what's at stake.

Pediatric psychiatrist Donald Winnicott contends that not only is *being* more important than *doing* in regards to psychological health, but that *being* must precede *doing* in order for *doing* to have significance:

> "*Being* is at the centre of any subsequent experience in life. In fact if the individual has not had the opportunity to simply *be*, his future does not augur well in terms of the emotional quality of his life. The likelihood is that this individual will feel empty."

> "Now I want to say: 'After being–doing and being done to. But first, being."
>
> "The ability to *do*, therefore, is based on the capacity to *be*. The search and discovery of the sense of self, in the context of therapy, is all to do with finding an identity."
>
> "It cannot be overemphasized that being is the beginning of everything, without which *doing* and *being done to* have no significance."[2]

Being, according to Winnicott, is more important to mental health, and is ironically the thing males are most encouraged to forego in favour of doing. You'd better not relax and simply be – there is work to be done!

The trend of separating boys and girls along these lines starts early. The boy gets a dump truck and a Bob the Builder toolkit, and the girl receives a Be Yourself Barbie™. Through the person of Barbie girls learn the experience of 'being' in a doll's house, and being relaxed, being pretty, being ugly, being among friends, being at a cafe, being married, or being happy, sad, jealous or vain. That's the psychological cloth little girls are cut from.

The first question we ask a boy is "What sport do you play," or "What kind of work do you want to do when you grow up?" Men are taught to be action figures who work, do the wage earning, do the repairs, or do their girlfriend. As long as they are doing something, we assume they are in their rightful place.

But *doing* can only return value if the person first exists. If he doesn't feel like he exists on a basic level, all efforts in doing have no meaning because there is no 'me' doing the doings. In that instance all doing becomes futile because it never leads to a sense of me-ness. Or, if doing does provide a momentary illusion of me-ness, it all vanishes the moment activity stops. When all is still, with no future plans, many men are swallowed by an existential void.

With the modern mandate that men *do* and women *be*, there's a dearth of male models for how to be. So for the purpose of this article lets revive a classical source illustrating what men have lost and why we would do well to rediscover it. For our purpose let's consult the 2,600 yr old sage Lao Tzu, who cultivated a philosophy of non-doing (Wu wei), defined as follows:

> Wu wei (Chinese: 無爲) is an important concept in Taoism that literally means non-action or non-doing. In the Tao te Ching, Lao Tzu explains that beings (or phenomena) that are wholly in harmony with the Tao behave in a completely natural, uncontrived way. The goal is, according to Lao Tzu, the attainment of this purely natural way of behaving, as when the planets revolve around the sun. The planets effortlessly do this revolving without any sort of control, force, or attempt to revolve themselves, instead engaging in effortless and spontaneous movement.[3]

Being aware of the importance of the doing/being dichotomy, one of the first books I gave my son, at the tender age of 10, was a children's version of the Tao Te Ching by Lao Tzu. We read it together and enjoyed some interesting discussion about the wise old sage, especially about his contention that the wise man "Acts without doing" — What did it mean? I'm not entirely sure if we got the meaning right, but we decided it meant to 'act' in the way you want to act, without 'doing' what others demand or expect from you.

In another translation the old sage says, Act without doing; work without effort. In each of these phrases he seems to be saying let it come naturally, let it arise out of *being*, and not from pressures from the outside world.

None of this is to suggest that boys and men shouldn't be active in the world. The good news for men seeking that greater balance is that you don't have to sacrifice doing in the process. Most men really MUST do in order to be healthy. But there is a distinction to be made here between healthy and unhealthy doing.

It's one thing to act from a spontaneous sense of self – a *being* self – and yet another to operate from compliance with the wishes of others because you were raised on a narrative of utility. Those living the narrative of utility must first become conscious of that before giving themselves over to an exploration of *being*, and if that consciousness is not first achieved then it's guaranteed that your attempts at *being* will be interrupted by internal guilt or by shaming from those who have most to lose from you walking off the plantation.

As per Lao Tzu we don't stop doing but rather become more conscious of our motives so that doing can emerge from a different center – not gynocentric duty, but conscious choice grounded in the ability to *be*.

One of Lao Tzu's main disciples Chuang Tzu elaborates the topic:

> Heaven does nothing: its non-doing is its serenity.
> Earth does nothing: its non-doing is its rest.
> From the union of these two non-doings
> All actions proceed,
> All things are made.
> How vast, how invisible
> This coming-to-be!
> All things come from nowhere!
> How vast, how invisible-
> No way to explain it!
> All beings in their perfection
> Are born of non-doing.
> Hence it is said:
> "Heaven and earth do nothing
> Yet there is nothing they do not do."
>
> Where is the man who can attain
> To this non-doing?[4]

Remaining with our fictional character Lao Tzu a little longer, let's consider the traditional tea-making ceremony legend says he helped to found. Just as Barbie is famed for her tea parties in which she teaches girls the arts of being among friends, Lao Tzu is credited with the first Chinese tea ceremony, a ritual centered in the experience of stillness and presence.

We may be reluctant to talk about a 'Tao of Barbie,' with her narcissistic overtones, but the tea drinking ceremonies of the Chinese and Japanese cultures deserve a nod to the noble Tao of Lao Tzu.

Taoism, like most ancient religions, talks about the balance between work and repose. By way of contrast, while Barbie also teaches girls that a work/life balance is possible, it's not certain that Barbie takes the work part of that equation very seriously.

To summarize, a common element running through all narratives about men is *doing*. We hear it in phrases like "All work, no play," "Don't just sit there, do something!," and "No rest for the wicked." Men slave for gynocentric culture as its saviors, fix-it men, martyrs, protectors, laborers, office-workers, and heroes – all narratives based on doing. But there's good reason for men to break from the cycle of servitude to enjoy some moments of being – being for themselves.

It's time we stopped for a cup of tea: ritually made, mindfully sipped, with or without friends, and without a need to watch the clock for the next round of work.

References

[1] On Dr. Warren Farrell's website the phrase "Women are human beings, men are human doings" is credited to his book *Women Can't Hear What Men Don't Say*. Elsewhere he explains: "I think the source here is yours truly. In the late 1960s, when I began speaking in this area, I used to say this. Although I've checked a dozen books of quotations and believe I created this, I wouldn't bet my life on it." (p.275).

[2] Jan Abrams, The Language of Winnicott; A Dictionary and Guide to Understanding His Work (1996)

[3] Wikipedia: Wu wei (June 5, 2015)

[4] Thomas Merton, The Way of Chuang Tzu (1965)

Printed in Great Britain
by Amazon